AWAKENING HUMANITY

AWAKENING HUMANITY

Our Place Among Extraterrestrials and Angels

BETH GEER

Cogent Publishing NY
Imprint of The Whitson Group, Inc.

Published by Cogent Publishing NY
Imprint of The Whitson Group, Inc.
3770 Barger Street, Unit 604
Shrub Oak, NY 10588
USA
(845) 528-7617

A Course in Miracles material used in this book comes from the ACIM Third Edition published by the Foundation for Inner Peace (www.acim.org).

ISBN: 978-0-925776-13-6
1 2 3 4 5 — 26 25 24 23 22

CONTENTS

FOREWORD
Jon Mundy

The Creator of life, the Source of everything that lives,
the Father of the universe and of the universe of universes,
and of everything that lies even beyond them would you
remember. —A Course in Miracles Text-19.IV.D.1:4

Every now and then there comes a book that compels us to stop, stretch the mind, look at something that transcends limitations, and move beyond what we've known before to something we have long expected. Should we assume that consciousness is limited to one speck of a planet, in one solar system, spinning around one star in one galaxy? Astronomers don't know how many stars there are in the two trillion galaxies they can see so far. One interesting development is that they have identified water on at least one planet outside our solar system.

Awakening Humanity is such a book.

I met Beth Geer and her husband Paul at a retreat in the mountains in North Carolina in the fall of 2019. We share similar backgrounds in that we both grew up on ancestral farms in the Midwest. Beth's spiritual background is rich and diverse. She has had a multitude of psychic, paranormal, and profound spiritual experiences throughout her life, beginning when she was very young. She is an active student of the book *A Course in Miracles* (simply called "the Course") which consists of a complete self-study thought system. Beth not only read her way through the voluminous book, she re-read each section over, again and again, carefully studying each idea as she went through the Course. In addition, Beth has also worked her way through the 2,100 pages of *The Urantia Book*.

Most of us are, much of the time, more tuned in to messages coming from our egos than from our Higher Self. The goal of *A Course in Miracles* is to help us turn down the volume of the ego, so we might then be able to be more receptive to messages from within. In this regard, through study and practice, Beth has learned how to become a better listener in order to "hear" that Inner Voice that is ever-present and immediately available to everyone all the time. It is a matter of tuning our receiver to the right-minded station. Our Higher Self is never absent. It is we who create the static that keeps us from hearing.

> *Consciousness is the receptive mechanism, receiving mes-*
> *sages from above or below; from the Holy Spirit or the ego.*
> —A Course in Miracles C-1.7:3

From 1969 to 1979 I taught classes on "Mystical Philosophies" and "Consciousness Expansion and Religious Experience" at the New School University in New York City. It was an exciting time and place of expanding liberality, particularly among the young. "The Dawning of the Age of Aquarius" topped the music charts as it blared out from boom boxes supported on the shoulders of young men with long hair walking through Greenwich Village. The musicals "Hair" and "Jesus Christ Superstar" were drawing large crowds on Broadway. As thousands gathered in Woodstock to revel in new-found freedoms, a shift from the status quo took hold. This period of time truly marked a beginning of a shift, however small, in our dormant conscience.

The seeds of this dawning of the Age of Aquarius so many years ago has grown into what now seems to be an awakening of what has become the birth of a radical sea change that continues to challenge the status quo. A growing number of people are delving more deeply into the vast potential of a Universal Mind of which we are all a part. This consciousness is expanding exponentially, both inwardly in our individual minds, and outwardly in the collective consciousness of humankind... and beyond that to the inclusion of the universe. As consciousness expands old ideas must, though sometimes uncomfortably, make way for the new. While attending houses of prayer and worship is now diminishing, we are seeing an increasing shift of minds expanding into an ever-growing deeper spiritual awareness that transcends organized, dogmatized, and stratified religion.

What's really revealing is that this expanding consciousness is not limited to the confines of our planet.

I first met Helen Schucman (the scribe of *A Course in Miracles)* in 1973 when she and Bill Thetford came to a conference sponsored by the Spiritual Frontiers Fellowship, where I was one of the speakers. It wasn't until two years later, in 1975, that Helen and Bill along with Dr. Ken Wapnick, formally shared with me the work they had been doing on what was to become *A Course in Miracles*, a book that has now been translated into 26 languages and has been read over the years by many thousands of students across the world. Helen was highly intuitive, religious in her own way, and given to vivid, often lucid, dreams and visionary experiences. Having known Helen I can say with sureness that she did not author the Course. She simply wrote down what she heard. Helen would take notes and then later read them to Bill, and he would type her notes onto what became the manuscript of *A Course in Miracles.*

It is not surprising that the Course was given to two psychologists at one of the top universities in the United States. The Course gives us a basic understanding of the psychology of humankind, explains how we got into the insanity we now find ourselves in, and shows us how to return our minds to sanity. Beth, in Awakening Humanity, now opens for us yet another door, letting us investigate a wholly new dimension in consciousness. Put simply, we find affirmation that life cannot be confined to one speck of a planet within the many trillions of solar systems. We are not alone in the Universe!

Dreams have always served as a means of contact between us, the unconscious, and a greater universe. The story of Joseph from the book of Genesis tells us of his interpretation of the dreams of Pharaoh. According to the Gospel of Matthew, the angel Gabriel appeared to Mary, the mother of Jesus, telling her that that which was conceived in her was of God. Likewise, Joseph, the earthly father of Jesus, was told by an angel in a dream not to be afraid to take Mary as his wife. Mohammed did not write the Quran; rather he said it was given to him by the same angel Gabriel who appeared to Mary.

Dr. Sigmund Freud, the founder of psychotherapy, spoke of dreams as "the royal road to the unconscious." Dr. Carl Jung, expanding on Freud's insights, pointed to a yet deeper collective consciousness that extends through all life: not just that of humans but of all life, including the collective consciousness of animals, insects and vegetative, life. As Shakespeare's Hamlet says to his friend Horatio: "There are more things in heaven and earth, Horatio, than are dreamt of in your philosophy."

Throughout history, revelations have come to receptive minds, which have made themselves even more receptive because of the depth of their study and meditation—minds that have, so to speak, "been in training." Dmitri Mendeleev (1834-1907), who developed the periodic chart for all the elements, said, after many hours of trying to figure out the periodic chart, "In a dream, I saw a table where all the elements fell into place as required. Awakening, I immediately wrote it down on a piece of paper."

Likewise, Einstein's Theory of Relativity came to him in a dream in which he was looking at an electric fence, watching cows jumping over the fence together. At the same time, a farmer standing at the other end of the fence saw them jumping over the fence one at a time. Their views of the same event were different because of where they were standing. It takes time for light to reach one's eyes. The mind must be in focus to see clearly.

Kenneth Wapnick, who in later years was to become the recognized master teacher of the Course, worked closely with Helen during the editing of the manuscript. In his book, Absence from Felicity, he describes how *A Course in Miracles* came to be. He explains how much of Helen's life was punctuated with vivid dreams and visions of a revelatory quality, from her early adolescence up through the whole of her life. She recorded many of her dreams, and we can read some of them in Ken's book. In her dream titled The Gentleman, for example, we find a description of a place where "the environment is perfect, but what one makes of it is their own affair." In like manner, in her dreams, Beth meets her guide, an extraterrestrial (to whom she gives the name Martha) who describes a place where "the environment is perfect."

The Voice for God never stops being available to every mind, all the time. To be receptive, we must learn to stop being projective. To see what is actually going on, we must stop making up the world. Now, nearly fifty years since the publication of *A Course in Miracles*, various "receivers" continue to open doors, allowing more light to come in—with works such as *A Course of Love, Choose Only Love...* and now Beth's book, *Awakening Humanity.*

The Gospel of John begins with the phrase: "In the beginning was the Word, and the Word was with God, and the Word was God." Before the big bang, before space and time and anything external, we have Mind—thought—the Word. What happens on the level of the mind or spirit is what matters most. Thus, the Course says,

> *If the mind can heal the body,*
> *but the body cannot heal the mind,*
> *then the mind must be stronger than the body.*
> —*A Course in Miracles* Text-6.V.A.2:6

As a result of her inner journeying, her vivid dreams and listening, Beth now reveals spiritual information to the world, passed on to her by Martha. Sit back, relax, and open your mind. Reading this book will take you on an amazing journey. I ran into some bumps, especially in the discussion of the Adam and Eve story. But let us not stop there. I interviewed Beth in one of my "Sunday with Mundy" podcasts, and the feedback was wonderful. Since that time, Beth and I have talked as she drives to and from work each morning and afternoon, and I have every confidence in her. Her story is compellingly believable.

Lovingly, Jon Mundy, Ph.D.
Author of *Living A Course in Miracles*
Publisher of Miracles Magazine

PREFACE

There is a change headed for this planet, and it involves more than just the human race. It's coming like a tidal wave, to wash us into a new way of living—a better, kinder, more loving way—but we can't do it alone. There are other beings living in other dimensions of time and space, on other planets, waiting for our receptivity for such a change; waiting for us to be willing to accept their help.

This book was received through my personal contact with one such individual, who reached out to me, offering just such assistance. She is here to help awaken humanity.

That being said, I will not ask you to accept what I am about to share with you. This is because the information I am offering is quite astounding and perhaps unbelievable to most. I would rather you think of it as a gift of knowledge, to be either accepted or rejected as you wish. However, please keep this thought in mind: If a gift is offered but refused, who then does the gift belong to? It still belongs to the giver, and the receiver is none the harmed because of their refusal. Therefore, if you do not believe or resonate with this material, you are entitled to disregard it and let us part ways as friends. No judgment or offense need come between us.

However, for those who do resonate with the words that follow, you have not come upon this material by accident. You are ready. It is the time of spiritual harvest. You are about to help usher in the awakening of humanity, and our Creator makes no mistakes in choosing His channels.

It is said that truth is often stranger than fiction, and so it is with the nigh unbelievable information I am about to extend to you as my gift.

That being said, I myself have lived a life of miraculous occurrences. I feel blessed to have come into contact with many aspects of the divine, including the Holy Spirit, whom you could call our collective "Inner Guide." I wrote extensively about this experience in my first book, "Awakening To One Love," where I relate the astounding conversations and knowledge that was shared between us.

I have also had contact with spiritual beings some refer to as extraterrestrials, in that they are from another planet, while others are from another dimension of time and space entirely.

My spiritual journey began at the age of five, when I once prayed to God asking if He could hear me—and the prayer was answered. This happened one night when I decided to kneel in front of my windowsill instead of lying in bed to say my memorized Catholic-taught prayers. There happened to be a cactus sitting on the windowsill, and it rested between my elbows as I closed my hands in prayer.

The next morning, as I opened my curtains to let in the sun, I noticed something quite remarkable: the cactus had three glorious pink blooms on it. I immediately reported this miraculous event to my family. They reacted with the appropriate excitement, albeit with one small explanation. The cactus must've been watered, for cacti often bloom overnight in the desert after a rain.

I accepted this explanation, but what still resonated with me was the timing of this event. My young heart felt no doubt that I was heard and answered by God. And so, this event began a lifelong journey of developing two-way communication between myself and our Creator.

Since then, alongside a practical college education to become a pharmacist, I have explored many aspects of the unknown. I studied the bible, numerology, astrology, tarot cards and reiki. I have also practiced meditation regularly since I was 16 years old and along the way my psychic and clairvoyant abilities developed.

A major leap forward on my spiritual path came in 2004 when I discovered both *A Course in Miracles* and *The Urantia Book* at the same time. I will not go into detail about either of them here, but suffice it to say, the information they contain has been the greatest spiritual gift I have yet received. These two voluminous works assisted my deeper understanding of nearly all my life's questions and were a springboard for my own personal contact with other life existing in creation, and God. My life has never been the same since—manifesting into a continuous, miraculous adventure into the unknown.

INTRODUCTION

Human beings, as a general rule, have always been afraid of the unknown. And yet we have an undying curiosity about the unknown that draws us to it, spurred by our sense of adventure. Fear always seems to lose out to the excitement of learning something new, but until we learn, we can sometimes react irrationally to what we do not understand.

That being said, I have had some remarkable encounters with beings not of this planet. My first experiences began in my early teenage years. I should begin by making one thing very clear, not a single encounter has ever been negative or caused me any harm. In fact, I look forward with great excitement to each new encounter. Each time I learn even more about who they are, what they want, and what our role is in the greater plan for our vast universe—a plan that both they and I agree is of God.

Many people may not have considered extraterrestrials and spirituality to be intricately linked, but they are. I assure you that their interest in our planet has nothing to do with our politics, climate or natural resources, although these things affect their greater agenda. Their primary concern, at least as far as my own observation goes, is our spirituality. We have reached a point where humanity is waking from a long, dark sleep, and we have many observers at our bedside-including extraterrestrials–waiting for us to join them with the rest of the universe.

Recently, individual E.T.s have begun to introduce themselves to me through psychic contact in order that I "get used" to them and come to know them more intimately. I feel they are doing this in order to make future open, global contact go more smoothly. I think the idea is that the more people who are mentally acclimated to their look and feel, the easier their "outing" will be. But most importantly, we are being implored to listen to what they have to teach us.

I will relay my early encounters first then move into what has evolved more recently, namely my contact with new races of beings; one of whom has agreed to collaborate with me in this work through clairvoyant, clairaudient and clairsentient communication; meaning that I can see, hear and feel her in my mind.

The purpose of her contact is to reveal spiritual information to the world through the dialogues that follow. Such information is something that, as she puts it, "Will help turn the world on its end. This is part of a greater masterpiece of information not yet fully revealed on your planet. We are but one small part, ushering in humanity's awakening."

Rest assured, I have taken careful notes of our conversations.

CHAPTER 1

My Early Encounters

My first memory of an extraterrestrial experience happened sometime in 1987, when I was about 12 years old. As I recall, I lay down for sleep one night, just as any other. The next thing I remember, I woke to find myself floating upwards in a tube of bluish light. I looked to my right, and there was a being floating next to me holding my hand. He was small, somewhere between only three and four feet tall—his head barely came up past my waist. His skin was a light bluish-grey, and he had large dark eyes, a thin line for a mouth and a small nose. I noticed his hands had only three fingers and a thumb and he was also wearing cloths; a one-piece, dark blue jump suit that fitted him closely like a second skin. He also had a strange golden insignia affixed to the left side of his chest. I peered at it closely for a moment, thinking it was a name tag, but it was not. It was a small, narrow emblem of some sort. It looked like a circle with a boomerang or "V" flying from right to left through the middle.

As I floated upward, I noted that though this situation should've been extremely distressing, I felt completely calm and safe. I looked down into the small being's eyes. His face radiated kindness, love, and compassion, though he had nearly no expression except a slight upward curve at the corners of his mouth. Love and peace simply emanated from him, and it encompassed me. I found the situation altogether enjoyable.

Once we reached the top of the bluish tube of light, we entered what was most certainly a spacecraft. As I looked around, I could see about twelve other small beings staring at me. As they realized who we were, they instantly turned back to their work. I could sense that they wanted to speak to me, but were instructed not to interact, lest they disturb my sense of peace and calm. This information came to me as an "inner knowing." No words were spoken.

The spacecraft was round and had a large viewing window, out of which I could only see stars and the dark night sky. There was also what appeared to be a control console encompassing the entire inside of the craft. Parts of it were lit with symbols and lights that had no meaning to me, while other areas were entirely dark.

My small companion and I approached a dark section of the console. He then telepathically asked me to place my hand on it.

I asked him why.

He seemed hesitant, almost embarrassed to explain to me that there had been some sort of oversight—through no fault of my own—in that they forgot to remove my "energetic signature" from the ship before I embarked on my current human life. This locked them out of some of their scientific functions. And now they were bringing me directly to their ship to unlock these functions because they were in need of access to them.

I then telepathically asked the small grey being how in the world did my "energetic signature" get into his ship to begin with?

He told me that I had been a part of their team before my human life.

I felt only mild disbelief at this but was not as shocked as I should have been because I was still immersed in a deep feeling of peaceful love and security.

I decided to just move on and asked the being where I was supposed to put my hand? The entire console was dark. There were no buttons or markings whatsoever and I was confused as to what to do.

Keep in mind, that this experience happened to me around 1987. I had never heard of a touch screen or seen a smart phone. If such technology existed, it hadn't become mainstream yet.

The small being gently took my right hand, spreading my fingers apart. He then carefully placed it on the console and the entire dark area immediately lit up with strange symbols and lights.

It seemed our task was now complete, and we re-entered the bluish tube of light to begin our descent.

The next thing I remember, I was standing in the middle of my bedroom in the dark. I turned on my light to check that I was alone, then ran to my bed, feeling disturbed; wondering about who I might have been in a past life and what the whole encounter meant. In hindsight, I couldn't say I felt fear or any form of trauma from this experience. The feeling of love and security that emanated from the small grey-blue being had left me with only the memory of a peaceful encounter. I had no grounds on which to justify any perceived malignancy from them.

I had a couple of other memorable encounters over my teen years. Once I found myself aboard a round ship similar to the one just mentioned. This time, there was only one being on board with me. His body was medium-sized, with sandpaper colored skin and large dark eyes. He was also wearing odd cloths; a white robe that concealed his body and a tall white hat. At first, it reminded me of the type of headpiece one typically sees the catholic pope wear but as I looked closer, I could see it was actually white wrapping that covered the long oblong shape of his head. I felt these coverings were being used to conceal his body so he would not look so strange to me. His hands were held in front of his chest in a curved, insect-like way, his long fingers reminding me of a praying mantis. I can also recall how he smelled; like a mixture of sandalwood incense and burnt matches.

We were flying over my hometown and the surrounding countryside. As I looked down on the beautiful night scene of the familiar river valley below, the being began to speak to me.

We leaned in close to each other, our foreheads nearly touching as I listened carefully, for I knew he was telling me something very important. His voice was soft and whispery; sounding very thin—as though he was not used to speaking. He was also using telepathic communication in conjunction with his audible words, which felt to me as though he was really trying to embed what he was saying into my mind, using both means of communication as a sort of "backup." At the end of the conversation he told me I would not remember his words until they were needed.

Next thing I knew, I found myself once again standing in the dark, in the middle of my bedroom. I quickly rushed to bed, deciding the whole thing was just a dream. Even so, I thought about the experience many times throughout my life, trying my hardest to remember what the extraterrestrial had told me. As before, I felt no fear during the encounter. The being felt like a dear old friend I had known for a long time.

On one other occasion, I woke to find myself aboard yet the same type of round spacecraft, flying over my family's farm. I could see by the moonlight the horses grazing in the pasture and my family's house and barns below. There were five small grey-blue beings on board, and I could sense they were young. They excitedly told me they brought me aboard just to show me they'd made it through training, and now had their own spacecraft. I was bewildered as to why they would share such information with me. It not only seemed strange but almost comical. Why were they telling me this? They then explained that I had had a hand in their training program in a different dimension of time and space and that one day—when my memory returned—I would feel proud of their achievement.

This encounter was short, and this time I woke up in my bed.

I am certain there have been more encounters than just these three. These are only the few from my childhood that I can remember clearly enough to describe. Many mornings throughout my teen years I woke with disjointed, vague memories of images of large dark extraterrestrial eyes and a faded sense of "having been away somewhere" during the night.

Before adulthood, I had one fully awake experience where I actually saw flying UFOs with another eyewitness. This happened in 1992, when I was 17 years old, while being driven home from a movie date by my boyfriend at the time.

We were driving on a country road with open fields on either side. The ridge of the river bluff was coming up in front of us and we were slowing down for the stop sign at the approaching "T" intersection.

As I happened to look out my passenger's side window, I saw a large light in the sky about 50 feet off the ground out in the field. I turned to my then boyfriend to ask him what he thought it was, only to see two more lights outside his driver's side window, only about 20 feet from our truck. The lights flew in tandem next to us until we stopped at the intersection. Then they shot straight forward at lightning speed and stopped to hover mid-air over the open river valley about 20 yards in front of us. The two lights then jettisoned at a ridiculous speed straight up into the air and disappeared. We then turned to look for the first light I saw hovering over the field to my right. It was still there, and we sat and watched it for about a minute before it too, suddenly shot straight up into the sky and disappeared.

It may be significant to note that the field where this sighting took place was owned by my grandparents at the time, and seven years later, in 1999, my husband (not the young man I was dating during the sighting) and I bought the property and built our house there, where we still live to this day.

After my teen years, all UFO and extraterrestrial activity seemed to come to a standstill. As I continued to explore all paranormal and spiritual phenomena as well as develop my ability to "hear within," I often wondered why such encounters had ceased.

Once during meditation, I was answered with, "To give you time to catch up to us." My impression was that the extraterrestrials were instructed to leave me alone while I deepened my "spiritual education."

There was no extraterrestrial contact for the next 22 years, from 1992 on until March 2nd, 2014. On this day I had one of the most remarkable experiences of my life. That night, I woke to use the bathroom at 4:00am and as I lay back down to go to sleep, I experienced an extensive waking vision which lasted for one hour. It was the memory of my past life during the time of Jesus. I was told by my Inner Guide that I was ready to have this memory returned to me. This happened exactly seven months to the day from when I first began the 365 Workbook lessons from *A Course in Miracles*.

After the vision, I lay there wide awake, my mind filled with thoughts about what I had just witnessed. It had been like watching a movie in my head and there was much to think about. It was not a life I had expected, nor a person I was proud to have been. It is not appropriate to share the story in its entirety here, as it digresses too far from the topic at hand. However, suffice it to say, I was a mean tempered, dishonest merchant/fisherman who found his way to God merely by experiencing a moment of eye contact with the man Jesus.

Once this remarkable vision was complete, I looked at the clock; it was now 5:00am and I had to get up in one hour to get ready for work. I figured there was no way I was getting any more sleep. Yet, the second I closed my eyes, I was dreaming.

I dreamt I was standing outside in the backyard of my current home, looking up at the night sky. Then suddenly, I saw a round spaceship hovering overhead. It sent me loving greetings, which I received within my mind, then moved on. Another spaceship took its place. Then came another and another; each somewhat different in form and style, but all bringing me the exact same warm, loving, greetings. I felt nothing but peace and love as I watched this strange procession unfold, but I was also confused. Why were they greeting me like this? Why were they welcoming me? Who were they?

After about twenty of them had passed overhead, the last one paused before disappearing like the rest. This last ship lit up its entire bottom with a beautiful collection of rainbow-colored lights. Then I "heard" a different message from this ship. It told me I was being welcomed back into the collective intergalactic consciousness of the universe soon, and they were all pleased to incorporate me when that time came.

What?!?

I woke up with a start. I was filled with a sense of joy at this message; I had a feeling of happy anticipation for this event, though I had no idea what such a thing entailed or when it would be.

There was no extraterrestrial activity again until six years later.

CHAPTER 2

An Official Introduction

On October 9, 2020 my husband, our two teenage children and I set out on a two-night backpacking trip along the Superior Hiking Trail, not many miles from Duluth, Minnesota. Not long after we began the four-mile hike to our campsite, I felt an intense sensation in my chest. It was like an explosion of love—I'm at a loss for words to describe it. It felt as though my heart was suddenly filled with a euphoric sunburst of loving happiness. This happened two more times before we reached camp, each episode lasting several minutes. I was certain I wasn't having a heart attack, in that, as a pharmacist and medical professional I had never heard of anyone describing a heart attack as pleasant, much less euphoric.

Once we reached camp, I noticed my resting heartrate had dropped from 70bpm to 65bpm. This was strange, as I'd been wearing a fitness watch for several years, and knew it usually took three to four weeks of increased cardio exercise to cause my resting heart rate to lower by five points. The only time my resting heartrate dropped down to 65bpm was during the two times I'd trained for half-marathons. This time it happened over a matter of hours, with no physical pre-conditioning at all.

I would not find out the reason for my "heart anomaly" experience until three months later, which I will share as this information unfolds later in my story.

That first chilly night, I snuggled into my warm sleeping bag and found myself instantly drifting off to sleep, after a rigorous first day out in the wilderness.

I then began to dream something strange and wonderful. A beautiful alien being appeared before me. Her form filled my view and the power of her presence was overwhelming. Not only could I clearly see her, but I could feel her as well. She radiated pure love; I felt as though I was in the presence of a truly divine being.

She was shining with an inner light that formed a halo around her entire body.

I lay there and began to observe the details of her face. As I did this, I became aware that I wasn't quite asleep; I could still feel my sleeping bag around me, and that I was lying on my back, facing upward. I realized that I was having a lucid dream—I was awake, but in a state where this glorious being could reach me while I was semi-conscious.

As I began to look closely at her face, she zoomed in to accommodate me. She had pale blue skin, that seemed to have a slight glow to it, as though her spirit shone from within. Her hair was straight, pure white, and hung down past her shoulders. She had bangs that were gently pushed to one side of her face. Her eyes were large and totally dark; and when I looked into them, they expressed only the deepest compassionate love I have ever felt. Her nose was small; no more than a hint of a bump, almost non-existent. Her mouth was thin, and the corners were curved up in a faint, but endearing smile.

She zoomed back out a bit and I could see she was sitting. The rest of her body was lean and thin-limbed but had our basic humanoid shape.

I could scarcely believe how beautiful she was, and even in my dream-like state, I marveled at how someone who appeared so different from humans could appear so glorious to me. Her beauty was her own and was incomparable to any human.

In addition to her captivating beauty, she felt ancient and wise to me, and with this thought she told me telepathically that she was only nearly halfway through her time in this body.

I then asked her name.

She replied with a thought, "You can call me Aya." (Pronounced "eye-yah")

She then wordlessly expressed to me that she was merely introducing herself and had been assigned to me as part of her work as a contact personality with humans. She indicated that this was only the initial introduction and there would be further contact as time went on.

She then completely disappeared, only to be immediately replaced by another, yet totally different, extraterrestrial being.

This one was male and if Aya had felt ancient to me, this individual felt beyond all time and wisdom. His skin was the color of sandpaper and he had an elongated head, that slightly curved off behind him. He had large, dark insect-like eyes, and looking into them, I felt as though I might disappear into his benevolence. I could not hold his gaze. There were only two small, faint holes for a nose and his mouth was just a thin line. His hands curved around in front of him like a praying mantis, ending in long thin fingers. He mentally explained that he was Aya's mentor; a being from a race even more ancient and advanced than hers.

I recognized him as the same extraterrestrial who delivered a message to me years before; the one who looked like he was wearing a pope-style headpiece and robes, with whom I had had an intensely personal conversation I had yet to recall.

He too, then instantly disappeared.

The vision had abruptly ended, and I lay there in my sleeping bag wide awake, wondering about what had just happened and what it all meant.

CHAPTER 3

An Extraordinary Extraterrestrial

My next encounter came exactly two months later, on December 9th, 2020. This one, too, started out as a dream, but was much different from the previous encounter.

I dreamt I was in the hay barn at my parent's farm, and there lying face-up, half concealed by loose hay, was a strange but beautiful looking being.

I took one glance at it and thought, "She's a female."

With this thought she corrected me telepathically, "No. I am a woman."

I instantly understood why she had corrected me; she was not just a female, as one would describe the gender of an animal; she was a woman; indicating we were the same in mind and spirit, though different in physical form.

I stared down at her and was stunned by her strange beauty. She had a smooth, hairless head, with a small dorsal fin lying flat on top. Her skin was a mottled color of a mixture of browns; like varied beach sand, that appeared to shift in shade and tone. It seemed her skin could change color just like that of a squid or octopus and the texture of it appeared equally as soft and smooth. I was mesmerized by the beauty of it.

Then I looked into her eyes; I scarcely have words to describe them. They had round black pupils, much like a human eye, but the iris was a translucent golden amber, filling in the rest of her eyes with a light that seemed to shine from within. Their warm glow conveyed nothing but gentle kindness and love.

My eyes traveled down her face; her nose was a thin pointed bump, barely perceptible, with no opening for air that I could see. It made her appear somewhat aerodynamic. Her face was smooth where her lips should have been and instead, she had a set of furry looking short tentacles hanging from just above her chin which moved slightly. Her mouth opening was not unlike what some sea snails have. I also noticed a set of three gills gently pulsating on each side of her neck.

The feeling she emanated was pure goodness and gentle strength. I felt she was courageous, loving and completely trustworthy in all ways. I also wondered how such a being, so different from how we humans look, could appear so mesmerizingly beautiful to me.

She then mentally communicated to me she was in desperate need of my help.

She said, "I need two things from you. I need you to hide me here, for there are people searching for me who want to capture or kill me. Second, I need water."

Setting all differences aside, I instantly wanted to help this gentle, graceful, kind squid-woman. "Okay," I replied without hesitation. "First let's get you more hidden, then I'll run up to the house and get you a whole five-gallon bucket of water."

"No," she said. "Don't waste any time hiding me further. Just get the water, but not in such an unwieldy container that it will slow you down. I need only a glassful, or even a wet towel will be sufficient. The amount is not so important as your haste!"

I then realized she was close to death, and the water would save her life. I hurried out of the barn, and an instant later I found myself handing her a glassful.

As she drank, her beautiful eyes met mine over the glass, piercing me with her loving, amber-lit gaze. The intensity of this interaction sort of "woke me up" and I suddenly became aware this was a dream, and I could feel myself still lying in my bed at home. Yet the dream did not end, but merely shifted into a more lucid mental state.

"So, I'm dreaming," I concluded. "And we're not really in my parent's barn, and you're not actually dying or in any real danger?"

"No, we are not actually in the barn and I am not dying or being hunted," she replied. "That was merely a dream-story scenario intended to engage you with me in an exciting and loving way; appealing to your sense of adventure and desire to help others. It was a way for you to instantly accept me and see beyond my strange and foreign form. By giving you a role that provided you an opportunity to "help" me, all fear of me was instantly replaced with love. This then caused you to feel comfortable enough with me to commence with this conversation. If you were to feel fear, our connection would be broken and you would have simply woken up instead of entering this lucid state of awareness, where I can communicate with you freely. The joy of helping through selfless service to another always triumphs over fear. You can overcome any fear through redirecting your energy towards some form of helpfulness. Fear separates, or disconnects, and love always unites, or joins. And so, I decided this was the most exciting and effective way to introduce myself to you and establish a loving connection. You enjoyed this small "pretend rescue-adventure" with me, yes?"

"Oh yes," I answered. "I enjoyed that a lot. The act of helping you was exciting and instantly made me feel like we're friends. So, what is your name?"

"I have no name pronounceable in your language. You may call me whatever seems to most closely match my vibration."

It took me only a heartbeat to "feel" her energy and say, "Martha. You feel warm, devoted, honest, loving, and strong, with a soft quiet beauty that to me, the name Martha conveys."

"Perfect," she replied.

I then desired to see more of her, and she showed me her long arms, that had fins along the forearms. She flared them for me to show they extended about 10 centimeters. She explained that they were used to push against water to swim backwards, as well as make sharp turns at high speeds. The rest of her body was not much shorter than an average human woman, but it was sleek and narrow, with no discernible female body parts.

She then showed me her hands. She had long webbed fingers like an aquatic frog, and an image came into my mind that her feet were the same; like giant scuba flippers.

Her chest was convex; the sternum protruded about four centimeters outward to form a vertical ridge, reminding me of the pointed prow of a boat. Everything about her seemed aerodynamic.

She wore a one-piece dark blue, skintight suit that had no sleeves, but then to my surprise the second I observed it, it disappeared.

"We do not need clothes, but only wear them to help others feel we are not so different," she said, in explanation of the sudden disappearance of her clothing.

"I see gills on your neck. Are your people aquatic then?" I asked.

"We began life in the great salty waters of our planet, and after mastering the sea, we evolved legs and the ability to breathe air through our gills, and then mastered the land. Next we took to the air and, finally, the endless space of our galaxy and beyond."

I was amazed to hear this and wondered how much water they had on her planet.

"Actually, our planet has less ocean than yours. Ours is just under fifty percent sea, but the water is one third more salty," she replied, telepathically. "You may ask me another question if you would like."

The first question that came to my mind was, "How do you raise your children? What is your family life like?"

"We women carry between two and four eggs in our abdomen. These are fertilized by our male mate at the time of family readiness. Then the eggs are excreted on the day they are ready to hatch. The younglings are all reared at the same time, along with other couples who are ready to begin a family. We time our births in "seasons," so our children are born in groups of the same age to create an efficient learning environment."

"How often does a couple have children?" I wondered. "How many in a lifetime?"

"We do this only once per lifetime, and it is optimal to have an even number of children so they can be paired for certain learning activities in the family unit. If a couple spawns more than once, it is greatly frowned upon and considered a selfish act. However, this occurrence is nearly non-existent; it is impossible for our births to be an accident. However, if a couple so chooses, and there is need, they can donate their pre-fertilized eggs to another couple to be carried and raised. Or, if they have an odd number, they can also donate an egg to another couple with an odd number, although it is rare to have only one egg or more than four."

And with that, I was suddenly fully conscious and lying awake in my bed.

I tried to reach out to her over the next few days but without success. I wondered when or if I would ever have contact with her again. At that time, I had no idea my next encounter with her would be another 32 days away.

CHAPTER 4

Telepathic Relationships

A month later, on January 10, 2021, I had been thinking about Martha during the day, wondering about her statement that her name was not pronounceable in my language. If the translation of her name was a problem, then how was it that we could communicate? If her name was unpronounceable, then wouldn't everything she tried to tell me be unintelligible? I also wondered where in the universe she was from and if she and her people would ever make physical contact with me or Earth in general.

The next morning I woke up at 4:30 and lay there wide awake, but mentally relaxed. To my delight, Martha appeared in my mind, with all the clarity of her previous contact with me. Without introduction, she began to answer my questions from the previous day, as though I had just asked them.

She said, "All communication is vibration that extends from your mind, outward through your thoughts. Words must first form as thoughts before they can be spoken. Telepathy is simply 'non-verbal thought.' But we must be on the same vibration in order to send and receive to one another. The only way you can receive me now is because your mind is in a vibrational state that is close enough to my own—one that is high enough or the most 'non-resistant.'

This idea may seem fearfully intrusive to you, in that there may be concern that others may somehow unwantedly invade your mind through their connection to yours. Overall, you must understand that no one need fear negative energy or 'attack thoughts' from anyone else; you can only be reached if you decide to be a vibrational match. Even so, such thoughts directed towards you by others cannot truly affect you, as negativity cannot extend or "give" anything of itself. Only love has the power to extend itself and thus has the ability to give. However, if you happen to perceive such negative thoughts in another, you can choose to release their vibration the moment you sense it. You do this by extending only your loving thoughts, which always raises your vibration. You will then be completely out of reach from any such unwanted communication. Therefore, the toxic thoughts of others cannot poison your mind unless you believe that this is possible.

This also works the other way around. If you want to communicate telepathically with me for instance, you must be in a state where you are receptive, which is a state of mind that is completely resistance-free or resting in total peace and tranquility.

As for our differing languages, yes, my people do indeed communicate with external vibrations, much the same as you do with speech. However, our language is more akin to the sounds of your dolphins and whales than human words. Since there is no word for my name in your language, you had to "feel" which one was the closest match. My name needed to be interpreted by you as a vibration you could put into a word. You offered me your interpretation as the name "Martha," and I agreed it matched my vibrational personality correctly.

All beings who are self-aware—meaning they can comprehend a power greater than themselves, from which they were created—have what you could call a Universal Translator. This Translator is bestowed upon all self-aware beings, and literally translates thoughts between creatures, so that communication can go undisrupted despite any language or physical barrier. Do you notice how we can communicate though we do not speak the same language, and neither are our bodies physically near one another? The Universal Translator is not bound by the physical laws of time or space. You have a name for this Translator on your planet. You yourself call Him the Holy Spirit. He is not only your Communication Link between yourself and your Creator, but also between each other as well as those from other worlds. You have even used it yourself to communicate with animals and plants."

I listened carefully to all this then asked, "So are plants and animals self-aware? Do they understand there is a Universal Creator? Because I have indeed, on occasion, been able to communicate with both animals and plants telepathically with undeniable success."

25

Martha replied, "They are not self-aware to the extent that you and I are, but they do have spirits that go on from their existence in the physical. The union you share through the Holy Spirit with all living things is what gives you the ability to link with them in mental communication. Though they do not possess the spiritual awareness you may have, in some ways they are more advanced than you. They understand that they are not their physical nature. On a subconscious level they know that if you cut down a tree or eat their physical form as sustenance, they are not truly harmed and do not feel "murdered" or angry over such acts. They know that their physical form is not who they are in truth, though this does not affect their surface desire to strive to live and procreate—which is a physical drive. What is destructive is any wanton suffering or needless waste associated with your treatment of them. And these acts are only destructive to you, not them. Destructive, in that loveless acts merely beget loveless experiences. Energy is always extending from you and reflecting back to you more of what you give."

"Understood," I replied. "Now what about my question regarding where you are from?"

"I am from a place as yet unknown to your world," she replied.

I couldn't accept that answer.

"Could you please try and show me somehow? So that I have a general idea?"

Martha responded by propelling me into a vision. I could see the earth, which zoomed out to show me the Milky Way and our universe. We zoomed out further, past many more galaxies, solar systems and whole other universes. Until at last, I was shown a beautiful green and blue planet that looked very much like earth, but with different landmass shapes. It felt far away indeed!

"Okay, I think I understand. Thank you," I told her. "Now can you tell me if we will ever meet in the physical? Will your people ever openly visit earth?"

"Such information cannot be given to you at this time," Martha replied. "Not because it is a secret, but because some of it is still unknown, and some information has to be carefully considered before it can be revealed. We must always consider if the information will help or hinder you. We will never reveal anything prematurely that will hinder your developing spirituality and delicate understanding of reality."

"What do you mean by "delicate understanding of reality?" Why is our understanding delicate?" I wanted to know.

"Because you are in transition from your current understanding of reality to a new understanding, and to reveal too much now could push you into panic rather than joy," Martha replied. "As just one small example, you do not live as though you understand that physical density is but one way for you to exist. There are many levels of physical density; for example, my people are only semi-physical. We are currently moving from one stage of density up to the next, which is why you can see light within my eyes. My spirit shines from within through my semi-physical state. Each level becomes less dense as you move upward in vibrational frequency, and each level of density has its own reality to go with it. In this sense, you and I do not exist in the same reality. I must lower my frequency to meet you in a half-way place. So not only are there multiple densities, but multiple realities or dimensions inside and outside time and space.

I am not presenting this information to intentionally confuse you, but rather to set an example of why it is difficult or can be untimely to share certain pieces of information."

I understood and couldn't wait to hear more, but at that moment without farewell, Martha disappeared.

However, this time, I didn't have to wait long to reconnect with her.

CHAPTER 5

Our Eternal Connection

Later that day, I wondered why Martha entered and exited our conversations so abruptly, without ever bothering to greet me first or say farewell. She replied to this thought on my drive to work, which also told me our connection was getting stronger—I no longer needed to be half asleep. Apparently, my ability to achieve the necessary "non-resistant" state of a higher vibration was improving. It was also the beginning of what would turn out to be an ongoing long-term dialogue between us.

For ease of both reading and writing, I will present these dialogues from here on in a playscript style format. Here is what was said:

MARTHA:

From my perspective such formalities are unnecessary. What you do not yet understand is that no-one ever "leaves" anyone—ever. In the telepathic relationship, everyone is continuously accessible to everyone—we are each only a thought away. It is no different from your conversations in the physical world. When you are at home or among your work friends, you do not begin each conversation with, "Hello, I am about to speak to you," or end with, "Well goodbye until I speak to you again in a few seconds."

No. Such introductions and conclusions to conversations with people in your immediate presence are deemed unnecessary and would be very odd. You simply begin speaking with whoever is nearby, and then cease to speak when finished. So, too, is it with the people on my planet through telepathy, and with you and me now. As far as I am concerned, when you direct your thoughts to me, it is the same as having a conversation with me as though I was physically present.

My dear, this is something your planet needs to understand—EVERYONE is a mere thought away, whether they are in your physical reality or not. Communication is always immediate and readily accessible through the mind. You just need to be tuned in properly. This is something your people will become more aware of as you spiritually evolve. Notice I did not say "learn to do," because you are already doing it all the time. You do this when you extend thoughts of love to one another and your Creator. And you do this when you grieve so deeply over deceased loved ones. Yet has it ever occurred to you that when they enter your mind, it is because they are reaching out to you? You think you can only extend your thoughts to them and that the conversation is one-sided, but I assure you, such contact is always both ways—and not always initiated by you. Pay attention to your thoughts and feelings!

As for you and me, keep in mind that if we are talking and you are called away to another task, I do not expect you to bid me farewell. Just as with a conversation in the physical, I will know when we are being interrupted and no other words need be spoken. We can continue our communication when you are no longer occupied by other tasks.

BETH:

So, everyone on your whole planet is in constant telepathic communication with one another? Doesn't it get noisy in your heads? How do you keep all the conversations straight? How do you keep any thoughts private?

MARTHA:

It is not how you think. We cannot barge into each other's minds uninvited. All it takes is a simple loving thought, extended to a particular person, and if they accept the feel of the vibration and decide to match it, communication is established. It is a more structured process than you imagine; however, it all happens quite instantaneously and naturally. Do you not feel this between us now? Have you grown accustomed to my vibration—the feel of me when I enter into conversation with you?

BETH:

Yes, you certainly have your own "Martha" feel. There is no question when you're present in my mind.

MARTHA:

> As for keeping any thoughts "private," know this: There are no thoughts we would not share because our thoughts are wholly loving and completely without fear or judgment. There are no private thoughts we would wish to withhold because every thought bestows love in the understanding of our unity in One Love. And only loving thoughts can be shared. Fear and judgment are what keep your human minds separate, a state we find to be very limited and filled with only suffering and loneliness.

And with that, our conversation was over, and Martha abruptly left my mind. I was left with only the loving feel of the connection I had just experienced with her.

CHAPTER 6

An Extraordinary Gift

The next day, on the morning of January 12, 2021, it happened to be my 46th birthday and I could feel Martha's presence in my mind as soon as I awoke.

MARTHA:

> I see today is your birthday, and I have two special gifts for you. I will tell you about birthdays on my world and have also been given permission to share with you when we will one day "meet in the physical."

BETH:

> I had no idea you could know such things about me! I never told you my birthday was today.

MARTHA:

> You thought it this morning upon waking, when you also noticed I was present in your mind. Thus, I shared in your "birthday thoughts." This is no different from if you were to speak out loud to me, if I were standing in the room, saying, "Today is my birthday!" Are you beginning to understand how our communication link works?

BETH:

> Yes, it's all very... intuitive. I have to remember to really listen to my feelings to know when you're there and become more aware of my thoughts. I hope I'm never thinking anything terrible about you when you're around.

MARTHA:

> Do not fear to have fearful or unloving thoughts. Remember: Only your loving thoughts can be shared or "experienced together" and yes, your feelings will tell you when I am present and when I am not. If you feel me, there am I. It would serve you well to do this with all people, especially your Creator. You all have the potential to feel the blessed Mind of your Creator and each other at all

times. We will talk more about this joyous state of being in depth soon, but for now, I wish to extend your birthday gifts to you.

BETH:

Yes, please do!

MARTHA:

Birthdays are the most celebrated event on my world. Children are precious, and celebrating life is a wondrous reason to gather together and take care to make extra fun. Since we are each born together in "seasons" or groups, we celebrate our birthdays with large numbers of individuals. There are special songs of great beauty composed and sung for one another, and gifts are given, though not as you understand them in your reality. Our gifts are of the heart and are felt rather than seen. We will literally walk through the day, sending "heart gifts" to all whom we pass by or seek out. The receiving of such a gift could be described as a sudden burst of great love within the heart that lasts for several minutes of your time. It is a sharing of an intense euphoric feeling of gratitude and mutual blessing. Nothing brings us greater joy than giving such gifts to one another!

BETH:

That sounds truly amazing. I wish we could do that to each other here.

MARTHA:

One day you will. Our conversation here is part of bringing about the awareness to welcome such a step in your spiritual evolution. And I would like to point out that you have already received such a gift from me once before, on the day of your backpacking trip in the wilderness.

BETH:

(Gasp!) You mean three months ago back in October when my family and I were backpack camping up north? When I felt those sudden surges of love in my chest? That was you?

MARTHA:

Yes. Your heart chakra was being adjusted in order to better receive the vibration of a higher dimensional being. You could say you were being "tuned in to the Martha channel" in order to be able to channel or hear me now. I was setting you up on my wavelength so to speak. And since love always strengthens, by doing so, your physical heart alongside your heart chakra became stronger for a time. This manifested in the lowering of your resting heartrate to that of your being in peak condition. However, all this could not be done without you yourself being receptive and willing for such an adjustment to take place. Your lack of resistance to your rising vibration allowed you to meet us partway. Rather than feeling fear at such an unusual new sensation, you embraced it, allowed it and even encouraged it. You have learned to let go of fear of such things through a combination of meditation and spiritual desire. Meditation is a deep form of prayer if used correctly. It is communion with your Christ-center, the pureness of your heart of hearts. It is to desire that only love be given and received. It is a prayer that is always answered, because it asks only for your truth to be made real by you, for you are only love. You have been attempting to do this through your recent meditations. We will speak more on this in the next chapter.

BETH:

Oh, I really love what you've shared here. Thank you for this first birthday gift!

MARTHA:

Now, about the second part of my gift to you: Revealing the day we shall meet "in person." I will be there for your coronation day. You will meet me then.

BETH:

My coronation day? What day is that? What is that?

MARTHA:

Your coronation day is what we call the translation of your identity from your physical form to a higher vibrational frequency. It is the day you rise in density to a level where you need not come into a physical body as you are now—ever again. Your lessons on this plane of existence will be complete, no further choices need to be made. Your decision to be as you are created becomes absolute. Such an event is celebrated in the higher, non-physical eternal realms above this one and we call it your coronation day. It is the day you fully exchange time for eternity; it is the moment you are consecrated to the eternal path of love and light—the goal of all creation. In your language, the word coronation means "to crown." It is truly your crowning achievement—the acknowledgement by all creation that you have been crowned sovereign over your eternal destiny. Put simply, it is the recognition of your awakening. Never again will you fall into the sleep of forgetfulness of Who You Are. It is something all beings with the power of decision between the physical and eternal will someday choose. Everyone's eternal destiny is inevitable, though you can delay it as long as you wish. Overcoming this delay is why I am here now, having this conversation with you, helping to awaken all humanity.

BETH:

How exciting! I'm looking forward to that event already. Can you tell me when it will happen?

MARTHA:

Absolutely not. First, because I do not know exactly when this will be for you. Second, even if I did, I would not reveal—and ruin—the happy surprise of something so wonderous and joyous.

BETH:

So how do I hasten the learning of my lessons on this plane of existence? I want to overcome as many delays as possible so that day can arrive more quickly.

MARTHA:

You already know the answer to that question. You have read books that explain it in great detail, and you have even written and published your own book about it. You are here to learn to extend forgiveness. This is what every moment in life is about. Learning to extend forgiveness. This is how the world is overcome with love.

BETH:

Can you explain then, in your words how forgiveness works? Half the time I'm not even sure when I'm doing it, or if I'm doing right.

MARTHA:

To truly forgive, not as your world teaches, but as some of your spiritual truths share, means to overlook. It is to look directly at the world you see, and know it is not all there is— it is not the real world. It is to not hold this world responsible for your happiness. It is to relinquish your current reality—to let go of all of your emotions tied to it—and seek to know the truth of what creation is—without your judgment laid upon it. And though only a subtle shift away, the real world truly is, a world of difference from the one you are in now.

There is a simple formula you can follow to ensure you understand and use forgiveness properly. It can also be called the "formula for inner peace." You know what it is, though your belief and experience of it is intermittent.

BETH:

Yes, I do know what it is, and yes, I've found it only works when my heart and mind are both in the right place. I will share it: First, you extend forgiveness, which is to release your mind from the idea you are a mere body and to release your mind from any perceived outcomes to situations involving the body—in essence, you overlook everything associated with the body. This induces a miraculous state of mind, where once you are released from the ideas associated with being a body, anything is now possible. A miraculous state of mind is simply the recognition you have indeed released yourself from your bodily ideas. You will know this has been achieved by the state of inner peace you feel. You will feel free of all inner conflict. Inner peace is direct evidence of miraculous thinking, which is then reflected back to you from the miracle you have extended. This then brings you full circle to an inner state of Atonement, which is the inner state of both knowing and feeling your peaceful Oneness or At-one-ment with all creation. So, the "formula for inner peace" goes as follows:

Forgiveness + Miracle Mindedness = Atonement

In other words:

Overlook everything outside you and notice only your Divine connection within + feel the release such overlooking brings = Total and complete inner peace with all things or a state of Oneness.

MARTHA:

Yes, and again, this peaceful state of mind is the goal of all true meditation. As we discussed in the previous chapter, it is the highest form of prayer. Once you have truly forgiven the world and all things associated with it, not only will you feel a deep abiding peace with regard to whatever it is you look upon, but the whole situation will actually become absurd to you—comical even. You will literally laugh in the face of adversity once you understand the truth. The world and all its inhabitants will lose their "seriousness" to you. You will cease to take life so seriously, knowing it can have no real effect on you, given it is not your true reality. It may appear that you are losing your mind, but you will actually have found it at last. Understand, you will not become indifferent to the world, but rather, you will see no difference at all between yourself and others in the world. You will gain a sense of love and unity with all creation like never before. Such a feeling is the Atonement or sense of being "at one" with all creation.

BETH:

Wouldn't such a state of mind cause people to just give up on life, knowing it's not "real?"

MARTHA:

No. Rather than "checking out" the mind will at last be fully "checked in." Your engagement with creation will become fully realized as your full awareness of your power to create will be restored and made conscious to you. Believe it or not, you will begin to have fun living here, knowing that a joyful experience of this reality is literally at your fingertips—a mere thought away from shifting to greater and greater vibrational heights of loving adventure.

BETH:

Sounds easier said than done.

MARTHA:

Yet, if you knew what waited for you, you would not hesitate to drop your feelings of attachment to this world in a heartbeat. You would hastily come into a state of total and complete forgiveness of this reality, instantly.

You fear to lose everything in this world through letting go, but you have the whole universe to gain. You have a host of family as well as amazing and wonderous experiences waiting for you in the grand superuniverse of all creation and we are but a mere vibration away. With that being said, how difficult can the choice for inner peace be?

And with that, Martha was gone. I thanked her for my lovely birthday gifts and though she did not reply, I knew that she received my gratitude.

CHAPTER 7

Meeting Across Time and Space

BETH:

How did you come to find me Martha? Why did you come to me?

MARTHA:

Do you recall that a few months ago you began to meditate differently?

BETH:

Yes. I've been trying to meditate all my life, but in the last two months I've been doing something different. I've been extending love *consciously* out into the universe, trying to feel myself become one with all living things out there. And each time I do this, to my surprise, I feel a host of beings spread out across unimaginable distances reflecting love back to me in return. I truly get a sense of countless presences all acknowledging my message of love to them. Then I take the love they are returning to me, and channel it down into the earth to be taken up by the plants, which then extend the love of the universe to all the animals and people on our planet. Then I imagine love extending from all the people, animals and plants back out into the universe, completing the circle. It is truly an amazing process and I absolutely love engaging in this type of meditation. It gives my mind something to do other than wasting time fighting back thoughts I don't want or searching for some elusive state of "mental emptiness."

MARTHA:

Did you think such a grand display of love would go unnoticed; that your call would go unheard? You were consciously choosing to move into the state of Atonement, and I assure you that what you are doing is real, and with real effects. Out of the countless numbers of beings who were able to sense your vibration of love being extended to them, I was among them. And I recognized we had similar callings.

On my planet, you could say my occupation is that of one who assists others along their spiritual path to love. It gives me great joy to help accelerate love in others. I am, in essence, a teacher of love.

Your planet is quite well known in the grand universe. It is known because of its lack of love—the state of limitation in which you now live. I recognized what you are trying to do. You are trying to teach love in a loveless place. And so, I was granted permission to join you in that task. So here I am, at your service.

BETH:

I'm speechless. I'm beyond all gratitude. Thank you, dear friend, I look forward with great excitement to whatever it is we do together. However, I would not say our planet is totally without love. I think there is love here, though it can be sometimes hard to find.

MARTHA:

I am not talking about your current definition of love, which is as your world defines it. Your world confines love to a form of attachment to the physical. In this sense, your world is indeed "loveless," in that no one walks the earth in full awareness of your non-physical interconnectedness to all creation. You do not feel your wholeness through unity with all living things, each other, and especially your Creator. If any such person did walk the earth with this awareness for any length of time, they would instantly be translated into a Heavenly existence just a single dimensional shift inward.

There is a joy beyond all expression when in a true state of love—in fact it is the only state of love—which is the natural state of creation in what is called Heaven. From our perspective, to live as you are all living now, in your seeming "separated state" of unawareness of the Love all around you, is hell.

Do you know that when you meditated with the thought of extending your love to the universe, it crossed time, space and also other dimensions?

Love knows no bounds. The only barrier to Love's Presence is your refusal to acknowledge it. But to lift this barrier you must change your beliefs about what love is and who you are in relationship to it. Your thoughts and beliefs are your power. Your thoughts and beliefs literally hold entire worlds and different realities away from your own awareness.

BETH:

Okay, so how do we lift the barriers to Love's Presence? Just through forgiveness? Constantly trying to "forgive" or "overlook" everything in my physical reality all day long sounds like a constant chore.

MARTHA:

It needn't feel like a strain. If there is strain, you are not achieving true forgiveness. Forgiveness is a way of loving the world, and love causes no strain at all, for it is your natural state of being.

There is another way of looking at forgiveness. It is also a state of being truly in the present moment. This is yet another awareness you can use to activate the vibrational frequency of love through which forgiveness flows naturally, and without any effort at all.

BETH:

This reminds me of a meditation I wrote not too long ago. It was about how to just let things "off the hook," and bring yourself back into the present moment where peace is found.

MARTHA:

Yes, that is a very effective meditation. A thought process it would be good for us to share here, as a teaching tool for others.

BETH:

I don't feel right sharing my own work here. I don't want to disrupt the flow of our conversation.

MARTHA:

We needn't disrupt anything. We can present it through the lens of our conversation as we are already doing here. I view this as a joint collaboration. Are we not both teachers of love? And you are not without knowledge. Therefore, it is my desire that we both share through our own experiences and perspectives in this dialogue. Let us together explain the thought process through which many may find benefit as an effective tool against those thoughts that inhibit their spiritual growth.

BETH:

Alright, I'll let you share it as you understand it in the next chapter. I would like to hear your take on things. Besides, I've found you can explain concepts much better than I can anyway.

Before we move on though, I have an interesting observation. The meditation I wrote a while ago regarding how to "let things off the hook" was ocean themed. I find it interesting that you yourself are an aquatic ocean type of being. Was this meditation inspired by you before I even knew you existed?

MARTHA:

(Gently laughs) No, my dear. I did not directly inspire your "nautical-themed meditation," but it was inspired by our Creator. Did Jesus himself not say we will all one day become "fishers of men?" So, it seems that our Creator, being consistent, appears to be continuing with this theme here.

As for my "aquatic form," remember, this body is only semi-physical. My inner light shines forth from my eyes. The Great Rays of eternal light are my true essence and identity. However, that form is not practical when communicating with forms such as yourself. My full "light body" would be mildly disconcerting and less relatable to you. I use this form for all my teaching work, and it serves me well. I will one day leave it behind entirely when this stage of my living is complete.

However, the fact that I am an aquatic being does have significant symbolism here. I come to you now, as representation of an aquatic people which is befitting of your planet's entrance into what you call the "Age of Aquarius"—a water sign for the fluid-minded state required to usher in the age of enlightenment. A state of mind I am committed to helping your world to achieve.

BETH:

That makes perfect sense. Supposedly, we just entered the Age of Aquarius on December 21st, 2020. But speaking of the ocean, I actually find it terrifying. It's so vast and filled with deadly creatures we barely know anything about. I don't really like the restless incessant sound of it much either. There are also the waves and strong currents that can drag you out to sea and the potential for tsunamis. All of it feels uncontrollable and scary. I find the quiet stillness of a mountain forest much more preferable—and safer. I really like to keep my feet on land if you know what I mean.

MARTHA:

All fear stems from a lack of understanding; you fear the unknown. Fear dissolves in the light of knowing. Therefore, do not fear to have your fears dispelled. They can be "let off the hook" most gently and quietly.

CHAPTER 8

Let It Off the Hook

BETH:

I'd really like to be able to gently allow all my fears, anxieties and worries simply be quietly and gently dispelled by the light of truth. Please give me your take on how to do that, and also explain what I'm doing wrong. Because I know I'm doing something wrong at least sometimes, because what I'm currently doing only works sometimes. I'd like to know how I can improve so that I can effectively recover my inner peace consistently all the time. No matter what seems to be happening in my life now.

MARTHA:

Alright then. Let us see if we can do that for you, and for many others, because yours is the same problem as everyone else's. You are all much too "hung up" on every single detail of this world; from the number of weeds in your lawn to the loss of a loved one. The range is wide and endless over which your minds can find things to trigger a sense of loss or deprivation.

Anything that holds you back from feeling your greatest joy possible is indeed a "hang-up." It is a place in your heart where joy is literally blocked by such thoughts—joy truly gets stuck—and therefore it becomes impossible for you to feel it until you find a way to unblock or release those thoughts which seem to be causing the blockage.

It is indeed strange that you hold painful thoughts dearer to your heart than joyful ones. But given the teaching of your world, this is understandable. However, you will find it good to know this backwards thinking can be easily undone if you have even a small amount of willingness to try.

The first step in removing the blocks to your joy, inner peace, sense of balance and well-being, is to look directly at what seems to be the problem. Name it. Write it down. Make a list, if you must. Think of everything in your life that bothers you or that you wish was different from what it is now. The only caveat is that all these things must have one thing in common: they must each cause you the same feeling. A feeling of being painfully "hooked" in the heart by the mere thought of it. This feeling need not be intense. The problem need not be judged as great or small, difficult or easy, excruciatingly hurtful or mildly irritating. A hook is a hook. Your heart, your feelings, will never be dishonest with you. Only your thoughts about such situations can be dishonest, but your feelings will always truthfully reflect your true thoughts. The important thing to do is consider anything that bothers you anywhere along the scale of discomfort.

Whatever thoughts you have selected, have you "hooked," like a fish on the end of a line. And just like a fish, you are struggling against the hook and it seems to be dragging you along against your will. It is your "hang-up."

Now sit with these thoughts for a moment. Look directly at them as raw and honestly as you can. Feel the feeling of your attachment to this hang-up. Again, for most, it will manifest as a sensation of discomfort in your chest. At times it can literally feel as though you have a hook through your heart.

You know you do not like this feeling. In order to cease feeling this way, you must let this situation "off the hook."

This can be easily done through the simple acknowledgement that you would like to be free of it. Let it dissolve in the knowledge that it does not own you. You are totally in charge of how you feel. No one else has any power over you. Feel your negative feelings fall away into nothingness. Cease to judge who is right and who is wrong. Cease to feel the need to control anyone else's feelings or actions towards you. Let go. Put it all down for just a moment. Whatever is causing you fear, strain or worry cannot take away the one thing that is wholly true about you: You are an eternal creation of God who is as indestructible as He is.

Now, let it come. Let all your fears come to pass in your mind. Let death, sickness, abandonment and loss in every form wash over your mind. Imagine the worst that could possibly happen to you.

Do you think any of this matters in eternity? Will any of these problems matter once you leave this level of existence? Will it change who you truly are as an eternally created being?

No. None of what you imagine is part of who you are in truth. All such problems are associated with the body and the body alone. You are not your body. Therefore, for the sake of your happiness, let all things associated with it "off the hook" for even a moment and you will find your peace.

You may think this is too easy; that you simply cannot just "let something off the hook" that has caused you so much struggle. Yet, how long should one struggle with their problems? How much time should you spend analyzing them? I tell you this, you will never get to the bottom of them. The problems of your world are a bottomless pit and this path will only lead you deeper down in vibration and experience.

You only need to notice your problems. That is all. Then let them off the hook. Once you do this, the solution will manifest itself easily and clearly in the shortest amount of time possible. In fact, at times, such solutions will be near instantaneous. At other times, events may first have to align themselves in order to bring about a positive solution. However, keep in mind, no amount of analyzing can change the past. But you can greatly alter your future through shifting to a new and higher vibration now through letting your emotional attachment to the problem "off the hook."

BETH:

But what if someone has done something terribly wrong to us? What if it's an abusive situation? Do we just let people walk all over us or even murder us?

MARTHA:

Not at all. Just the opposite in fact. By letting your feelings about the situation off the hook, you are cutting all such people and events loose—you have cut the line with them. No one and nothing can touch you in this state of mental indestructibility. They can even beat you, mock you and finally crucify you, and you will retain your personal power. This does not mean you approve of or support what someone else has said or done. It merely means that their words and actions have no bearing on your own sense of personal power. You know your truth remains true, regardless of what someone else says or does. You are simply reclaiming your personal power and while in this state you are most connected to your Inner Guidance, Who will direct you accordingly. You may be guided to take some form of action or you may be guided to remain still and steady as you are. All you are asked to do is get yourself off the hook and into the boat. You are rising above the situation and looking at it from your center of peace—the boat that floats above the violent sea that contains a myriad of fearful things and situations.

In truth, you are both the fisherman and the fish. You can choose to live life from the perspective of the boat, or from the perspective of the fish caught on the hook, struggling against everything you encounter.

Once you feel your peace, you have gotten off the line and are now in the boat.

Do you see how your hang-ups tether you to a line? You are not free when you feel such suffering. By holding onto your grievance, want or need, you merely set a hook in yourself which causes you to struggle.

The boat represents the present moment. It is where you will find your Source and Center. It is a place of quiet rest and joy. The boat moves forward in time, floating on the sea of all possibilities. And like time itself, it moves forward regardless of how many hooks you have set in your heart, holding you underwater.

You can cause the boat to move very slowly, through experiencing life as one difficulty after another, but you can never stop it entirely. Yet, if you let everyone and everything "off the hook," the boat will coast smoothly and speedily forward. You will progress much more quickly on your journey, and you will enjoy floating serenely on top of the sea of all possibilities, rather than struggling on a hook beneath the water.

Play with this practice. Have fun with it! Continue to let more and more things off the hook as you encounter them throughout your day. Make a game of it! Imagine all your hurts and wants and needs; the unfulfilled dreams, the desires of your heart that have been thwarted by one thing or another.

Then see how it feels to just let it all go. Let your attachment to all these feelings float freely away behind you. You are only making one small change. You are letting yourself off the hook. You want to be in the boat, serenely enjoying life as the fisherman, not the fish.

Therefore, every time you sense yourself as the fish on the line—and you will know by the tug you feel from the hook in your heart—let it go. Play this game of "catch and release" as often as you can.

You do not have to be tedious about this process. You can let the entire world off the hook in a single holy instant and it is done.

Feel no guilt over so easily overcoming your problems, which exist merely because of how you are seeing things. There is no guilt in being a fish caught on a hook, so long as you remember to let yourself go.

In time, you will notice you feel very good while in the boat. It is an inner place where the sun is shining, the water is wide and calm, as you glide smoothly across it, lovingly working side-by-side with God, your Captain; for He is there with you in the present moment of the boat.

This is where you always want to be. And if you happen to fall overboard and find yourself back on a hook, you can jump back in the boat with a single thought: "I do not want this feeling. I want to be happy and back in the boat, safe with my Captain. Struggling on the end of a hook is not worth the loss of my peace."

Then simply focus on something that will act as a life preserver; a positive thought to bring you back. You can use anything. You can focus on your breath or notice the soft feel of a warm blanket. Anything will do, so long as you allow it to uplift you even the slightest amount.

The goal here is to reach the feeling of love and even if it is on the most subtle level, you will have succeeded.

The deeper process at work here is that you are slowly learning to turn your thoughts inward and away from the world outside. You are not giving your peace away to that which will one day cease to be. You are giving your energy to what is timeless and eternal instead; you are giving your energy to God. And He will always increase what you give, and therefore He will increase the joy, peace and love you extend inward to Him. The key here is noticing the love you feel. Love is the vibrational signal you want to give to the world in order that it be reflected back to you. What you give, you will receive. This is your God-given power to create.

This is the process through which you help your Creator bring in the net from the sea of all possibilities.

It is important to keep your momentum with this process going—in the beginning, it may only last but a few moments before old fear-based thoughts creep back in. But as you practice more and more, allowing your thoughts to align with love for longer and longer periods of time, you will find that it builds momentum. Positive things will begin to manifest in your life, as your positive thoughts align your feelings with the vibration of your Creator; the vibration of Love.

This does not mean you can never have a negative thought ever again, for fear the world will come crumbling down around you. Quite the contrary! There is great power in "catching yourself" as the fish through noticing your fearful thoughts and remembering you do not want them. Do not try to solve them or force them to "go away" for this will only make them stronger. Simply notice your feelings and use your power of decision to focus your thoughts on something else; on something that uplifts you even a minute amount. Then you will have accomplished what many have spent lifetimes trying to learn.

In time, you will need no other positive or love-filled thought than this: "I am a creation of God. I cannot be destroyed or deprived of anything this world has to offer. I am that I am and have no need but to know my Unity with creation. In this knowing, all needs are thusly met."

As you practice, you will learn you are a powerful conscious creator; that your thoughts and feelings dictate your experience and nothing else.

Love is how you reach for your Captain, and as you do so, He will take your hand and pull you the rest of the way back into the boat, so long as you do not let go by deciding you prefer the feeling of the hook.

As you continue to practice, your life will open up for something new, something miraculous as you learn how to float above the world and its problems.

You will find you can go anywhere you want on the sea of all possibilities. All outcomes are now open to you because you have set no limitations on what can manifest. There is no hook set in your heart, blocking you from arriving at your happy destination.

It is important that you do not try to direct the boat; you must have zero insistence on any outcome to any situation or you will only find yourself back in the water as a fish on a hook—you will have fallen overboard. You are not the Captain, but the crew. Your job is to sit back, relax and follow your Captain's lead, Who's only order is that you do not insist on what should come in on His net. Do not insist on how, who, when or what will come to you as an expression of the joy you have asked for. Yours is only the task of trusting through peace and patience.

The Captain knows where to go on the sea of all possibilities. He casts a wide net to bring you what is most needed. For His net encompasses All That Is. All you need to do is help Him bring in the net. You can only help by being in the boat. Therefore, it is important that you notice the moment you get hooked and feel yourself going overboard. Release the hook the instant you feel any form of emotional discomfort, want or need and you will have released yourself as the fish.

If you are truly in the boat and remaining free of any insistence to any outcomes, you will notice that c will increase in your life, as the world arranges itself to meet your new, higher vibration. Act on these positive offerings; this is the bounty coming in from your Captain's net. All coincidences are signs of new opportunities manifesting in your life. Act on them. Move with them in the current, even if you interpret them as uncomfortable or fearful.

Indeed, there may be times the waters feel choppy and the waves will threaten to capsize your boat. You can calm the storm by simply remembering to let go of the hook. When you do this, the storm loses its power over you and the energy is transformed; now serving you rather than you serve it.

Never forget, you can climb back in the boat the instant you notice you are on a hook. You do this when you remember to replace fear with love, through whatever means is most comfortable to you.

Become diligent at keeping your mind clear of all unwanted thoughts, remaining in the boat with your Captain, as He casts His net wide on your behalf. Await what comes with peace in your heart, knowing it is already coming to you now. Do not let yourself worry about how it will come or what it will look like. Trust it will bring you only joy. Do not set a hook in your mouth through expectation, but release yourself through peaceful acceptance, here in the present moment, where all miracles are possible.

Now, sail peacefully along on the ocean of all possibilities without fear you will drown in it. Remember that the present moment is your ship, your thoughts are the winds that propel you forward, and God is your Captain.

BETH:

Again, you amaze me Martha with your clarity. Thank you for your help.

CHAPTER 9

Our Other Visitors

BETH:

Martha, what about the first two extraterrestrials I met during my lucid dream back in October of 2020? Will Aya or her mentor be involved with us?

MARTHA:

They will not be directly involved with our dialogues here. Aya has been assigned to you as a contact personality. This means, that when her people decide to make themselves known to you, she will be among the first you personally meet.

BETH:

In the physical? In this lifetime?

MARTHA:

Yes, to both questions.

BETH:

When?

MARTHA:

The process of intergalactic contact with beings from other planets has already begun. In 2023 it will progress in earnest as more and more beings introduce themselves, at first to individuals such as yourself, and then to larger and larger groups of people. This process of "open contact" will be gradual. The overall timeline for it to unfold can only be an approximation in that many things must come to fruition first; the spiritual harvest must be ready for reaping—meaning that the people of your planet must reach a mindset that is ready to meet them without fear or the desire to worship them. You must also reach a sufficient state of inner peace as individuals; a certain percentage of your population must elevate in consciousness to hold the higher frequency necessary for your realities to meet. There must be a closer vibrational match.

BETH:

Oh! That's wonderful to hear! And I have one other observation: Aya was glowing. How are my people going to react to her people if they all glow like that?

MARTHA:

You saw her as she is in her highest frequency. She and her people will have to lower their vibration some in order for the human eye to even see them—but your race is also rising to meet them. Each day, more and more of you are tuning into the frequency of love. Each loving thought helps collectively in unimaginable ways. And Aya's people look more similar to you than you think. Her people share genetic material with your race—you are related. You are truly family. In fact, you share genetic relation with more than a few intelligent races capable of interstellar travel, who will one day, in the not-too-distant-future, make themselves known to your people. Rest assured and set your fears aside, knowing they will indeed come in peace, with loving intentions. Many off-planet races will have appearances identical or very close to your own race.

BETH:

I am looking forward to that time with excitement! Can you describe any of the other races to me? What will they look like and who are they?

MARTHA:

As I stated at the onset of our communication, there are some things I am not able to reveal to you. Again, not because it is secret, but because the information must be weighed as to whether it will help or hinder your spiritual development. In this case, the beings themselves have their own plans for their revealment, and I am not permitted to interfere by introducing information about them prematurely.

BETH:

Okay then, I understand. Can I ask you something else then? Are you and I genetically related?

MARTHA:

No. My race was not involved in your physical development and we share no common genetics. Not only that, but I am not in your dimension of time and space. If I were to visit you in the physical, you would not even be able to see me. And if you were suddenly teleported to my planet, you would see nothing but a lifeless orb, though in my reality it flourishes with life. After your coronation, when you make your dimensional shift upward, you will see many things that you do not see now.

BETH:

Oh, I can't even imagine how wonderful that will be.

MARTHA:

You are correct. It is impossible for your mind to comprehend at this time. For now, you must be satisfied in simply knowing that this transformation is the destiny of all your people; the awakening of humanity is at hand.

CHAPTER 10

Mermaids Are Real—Sort Of

BETH:

I have so many questions I can't even form them into coherent sentences. I'll just throw one out here: What do you eat?

MARTHA:

My people, being first and foremost aquatic, sieve the oceans of our planet for microorganisms and nutrients. We do this through a membrane that spans across the upper region of our throats, located just above the area where our gills are located. The holes in this permeable membrane are very flexible. We can contract the holes down to that of a microbe or expand them enough to swallow a small fish whole—something the size of your minnows or young anchovies, although we long ago ceased to consume other conscious creatures for nourishment. Currently, our entire diet consists of a combination of micro-nutrients, energy from the source that lights our planet, and water. We need very little by way of physical sustenance in our now semi-physical state.

We can take in air either through this membrane or through our gills directly. This dual air intake was simply a result of our land adaptation. Once on land, it was more efficient to breathe directly through our gills, much the same as you breathe through your nostrils.

When we eat, we filter the sea water and also the oxygen that comes with it, so we breathe and take in food together, much as many of your fish do.

BETH:

That would be so strange to have a membrane covering my throat and eating and breathing at the same time through the holes in it.

MARTHA:

What do you think your epiglottal flap at the top of your esophagus is for? It can open to either direct air to your lungs or food and water to your stomach. And when you try to do both at the same time, you end up with food in your lungs, causing you to cough. We at least have a minimal choking hazard.

BETH:

Very true! So how many holes are in your throat membrane?

MARTHA:

How many hairs are on your head? How many pores are in your skin? We are similar in that our membrane contains thousands of openings.

BETH:

Oh, got it. So, once you evolved the ability to breathe air above ground, did you ever eat anything on land, as in animals or plants?

MARTHA:

We found the process of catching prey on land and removing the outer protective coverings such as fur or scales to be tiresome and time consuming. We also found the flesh must be cooked, and the bones dealt with. When one is finished with all this processing, we found there was not much left over for consumption and far more wasted than we could tolerate. And so, the efficient consumption of whole fish in the sea, with no preparation or waste what-so-ever to be the best food option, and as I stated above, we now no longer even need do that.

We did, however, find many plants to our liking on land and found that, when broken down and mixed with water, we could consume them much as we took in plant organisms in the sea. This added welcome diversity and new nutrients to our diet, which aided in our physical development as land-faring creatures.

BETH:

So, if you have a membrane across your throat, how do you talk?

MARTHA:

We force air through the holes to create the desired sounds we need to form our "words" which actually would sound more like music to you. Since we can open any number of holes simultaneously and in varying sizes, our language is quite complex. And along this same thought, our singing is beyond compare. One individual is capable of creating a song that would take a full symphony of yours to produce. Our notes can be held continuously as well, since we can take in air through our gills and push it through the membrane without stopping to take a breath as you must do.

So, can you imagine the artistry that goes into our celebration songs for one another? Combine such music with a "love burst" to the heart and you have a gift like no other. We relish composing new and beautiful combinations of song for one another. And when great numbers of us join in chorus, even the angels stop to listen—often adding their melodious voices to ours. And on occasion, we can engage all of Heaven in waves of glorious hosannas in praise to our Creator.

And know this as well, such great compositions of magnificent song are usually begun by a single inspired individual, who's melody is so moving to the spirit it becomes infectious and is taken up by every heart within hearing, spreading out into the cosmos and beyond. Therefore, never underestimate the healing power of what inspires you. Sharing your loving inspiration has tremendous effect on others and impacts your world and even dimensions you are unaware of.

BETH:

That's truly amazing! It also causes me to picture beautiful mermaids singing in the ocean...

MARTHA:

There is some truth to those myths on your planet. On rare occasion, when a sailor has been out to sea and sufficiently drawn into a deep meditative state due to the rocking of the waves and sunlight sparkling off the water, along with dehydration and malnutrition, we have crossed paths with your people.

Our dimension and yours have intertwined from time to time. But again, the conditions must be exact, and are rare indeed. I would not recommend trying it, because it usually means the sailor is close to death. He sees us, because his soul is half in your world and half in the next. And so, the few that chose to come back from such an experience will speak of how the "mermaid" tried to lure them down into the ocean with her song. We would do no such thing. They were simply seeing and hearing us going about our daily business, not in your world, but in the next vibrational dimension inward from it. In fact, many of your "creature sightings" and myths can be attributed to such dimensional overlap.

BETH:

Very interesting! You said something else interesting earlier, when we were talking about your diet. You said that it consisted of a combination of micronutrients, water and "energy from the source that lights our planet." What do you mean by source that lights your planet? Do you not have a sun?

MARTHA:

Remember, we do not live in your dimension of time and space. Our reality is no longer governed by the rules you must live by, though it once was. Our planet has an ambient light that comes from our Source, the Creator of all creation. We have no night, but a constant "perfect light" which is always present. It grows our plants and feeds our bodies by our taking it in through our skin and eyes. We are "fed" naturally by this light when awake and going about our daily tasks. It replenishes the energy of our spirits—you could call it "food for the soul." You would find it to be the most pleasant lighting imaginable, as do we. Does not your bible refer to God as the "Bread and Water of Life?" It is most certainly true in both spirit and body.

BETH:

I'm finding out lots of things to be true that I didn't expect. I also have a question about another comment you just made about what you eat. You stated that you, "long ago ceased to consume other conscious creatures for nourishment." What exactly do you consider to be "conscious creatures?" Are you completely vegetarian?

MARTHA:

There are levels of consciousness in all living creatures who take on an identity in the world of form. Level one: consumption. Level two: reproduction. Level three: self-preservation.

In the first two levels, the organism is basically responding to their environment through programmed physical reactions to it.

Their body triggers the urge to eat and if the food need is met, they next feel the drive to procreate or "make more of themselves."

The third level—self-preservation—indicates the development of the awareness there are "others" in their environment besides themselves and that they must take evasive action to avoid prematurely ending their physical life. This can either be the development of defense mechanisms, such as the ability to hide, run away or attempt to incapacitate other life forms if threatened. Another option some choose, if possible, is the development of a symbiotic relationship with another organism.

There is a fourth level of consciousness, and that is the awareness of a power greater than oneself. In the third level, the creature is not aware they came from another Source. As far as they are concerned, life began at birth and they created themselves. They do not worship or look to a higher power as their point of origin. Once a creature begins to realize they did not make themselves at birth and that there must be a power beyond the body which created them and which they do not yet understand, they begin the long universe ascent of the spirit and have the power to eventually remember themselves and their Creator. It is the path of ascension into unity and oneness with our Source.

Due to the possibility of the development of fourth level consciousness in third level consciousness creatures on our planet, we no longer seek them as food sources. Since we are gradually leaving the present vibrational level of our planetary environment as we transition from semi-physical to non-physical, we wish to leave the "playing field open" so to speak, for the next evolving creature. However, without the early years of our consumption of third level creatures in our development, such as fish, we ourselves would not have evolved to the place where we are now. It was a necessary step in our physical evolution.

That being said, we are not entirely vegetarian. Plants do make up the majority of our diet, but when we sieve the oceans of our world, there are many smaller organisms that are not plant-based which we consume. However, they have not yet achieved third level consciousness and take no evasive action against capture. As far as they are concerned, nothing else exists in their world except the need to eat and procreate.

Eventually, once we become entirely non-physical, the need to consume anything in order to perpetuate our lives will be obsolete. We will be fully sustained by our awareness of our connection to Source, or what you would call the power of God.

BETH:

So how is it okay to eat first or second level conscious creatures and not others? Shouldn't all living things be spared?

MARTHA:

It is actually to their benefit that we do so. Understand, if they went on through existence unchallenged, they would remain at first or second level consciousness. It is through interacting with us that they will gradually become aware there are other creatures in existence besides themselves. They will one day learn to take evasive or defensive action or form a symbiotic relationship with another creature, thus propelling them into third level consciousness.

Know this, it is through our relationships with one another that, too, propel us forward on our spiritual paths, from the very lowest consciousness to the highest, no exceptions. All things are continuously evolving towards greater awareness of what exists through their relationship with it. We are doing this together now—through our new-found relationship, we will help your people grow in awareness of what exists beyond what you now understand.

CHAPTER 11

Reality Can Be Manipulated

BETH:

What kind of homes do you have? Do the majority of your people currently live in the sea or on land?

MARTHA:

We need no organized shelter as you understand it. We need no protection from the weather, predators or other hazards. We own very little by way of physical possessions so there is no need for a "home" even as a place of storage. We do, however, have designated areas where we retreat each night to sleep and as a gathering place to be a family together. Some choose to do this on land and others in the sea. We have equal preference for both.

We need very little sleep. In fact, our need for sleep has nearly disappeared as we evolve into non-physical beings. Sleep is for regenerating the body and softening the spirit from the rigors of the day. If not for the reprieve sleep brings your people each night, you would die within 11 days, of both physical and mental strain.

As for requiring a home for physical shelter, there is no need for it as our environment is wholly peaceful and supportive without our need to take extra precautions. There are no storms, earthquakes or volcanic eruptions. There is no winter. The temperature remains constant, and when the gentle rains fall, what harm can that bring to a water-loving people? In fact, we relish the warm soft rain as it falls on our skin.

Our planet was not always this way. As our consciousness became more peaceful, so did the very environment in which we lived. As our inner world shifted, so too followed our outer world.

BETH:

But you said in one of our earliest conversations, and I quote,

"We began life in the great salty waters of our planet, and after mastering the sea, we evolved legs and the ability to breathe air through our gills and then mastered the land. Next we took to the air and finally the endless space of our galaxy and beyond."

How did you manage to master the "endless space of your galaxy and beyond?" When did you create spaceships or evolve through some type of industrial revolution to develop technology? MARTHA:

We took a path much different from yours in technological evolution. We began to understand how "things" in the world manifest or are "made" much sooner than your people have. There was no "industrial revolution." This is in large part due to our evolution in the seawater. It reveals much that air does not. You have also been greatly impeded by what is referred to as "The Lucifer Rebellion" and the long quarantine your planet has been held under. After 200,000 years, your planetary quarantine has at long last been lifted, and now there is much work to do to catch you up—which is why some call this time the "Celestial Speedup," the "Great Awakening" or "Quickening." The time for your speedy recovery is at hand. We will discuss this topic at length in a later conversation. For now, let us continue with the question at hand.

Water reveals the effect of waves of energy on physical reality much more clearly than air. You know this from your own experience. Your scientists have experimented with the effects of sound on water, witnessing the differing patterns created. Early on, we too could see the impact our sound vibrations had on the sand and water: harmonious sounds created pleasing cooperative designs, while discordant sounds produced chaotic or conflicting patterns. We found that harmonious or "unified" soundwaves, working together, arranged a physical reality that stayed together. It was the beginnings of our understanding of the benefits of unity versus separation.

We continued to experiment with such effects until we realized thought itself created an energetic wave that affected the world around us. We found that the vibration of love or the highest most giving, joyous, thoughts—unifying thoughts, such as feeling unified with our Creator—could produce wonderful results, arranging the sand and sea into most pleasing, harmonious forms. Using such thoughts, we could consciously create our own reality. We literally built what you would deem to be castles under the sea, all with the power of our thoughts. We could move the greatest stones and carve out whole underwater caverns to our liking. All without a single machine or tool, using vibration alone.

We then took our advanced learning onto land, and up there, at first, we required more substantial shelter than we do now, so we simply arranged the stone and ground to our liking—forming intricately beautiful abodes, using only the power of our thoughts. Not only that, but we could work very specifically, not disturbing a single tree or the most delicate habitat of any creature already living there.

All this was possible because the evidence of the effects of our thoughts on things around us was so apparent in the beginning stages of our oceanic environment. If not for the strong support and continuous reinforcement of our beliefs about the power inherently bestowed upon us through our Creator, none of this would have ever evolved. It is the belief such things were possible that gave our thoughts power. Do not underestimate the power of thought combined with belief. We have literally moved mountains with such power.

Gradually, we became interested in exploring outer space and what lay beyond our world. This was initially problematic in that we had no idea what we needed for survival or how such travel could be accomplished.

We reasoned that if objects could be moved with waves through thoughts, could we not simply "think" ourselves to wherever it was we wanted to be?

We found that we could indeed, but we could not take our physical body as it would not survive some environments on other worlds. We lost a few individuals this way. So, we perfected the art of distant travel by non-physical means through a form of "energetic projection."

BETH:

Is that what you mean by saying your people are "semi-physical"?

MARTHA:

Not quite. Some of my people have transitioned entirely into being non-physical and exist as "light bodies," while others of us are still physical, but with the light of the non-physical shining out through our eyes. Those of us who are fully non-physical beings are still visible to those of us who remain physical, though as non-physical they cannot perform some physical tasks. Likewise, those of us who are still physical, cannot perform some non-physical tasks. Let it be known, death of the body is entirely meaningless to my people. We simply change form and begin to exist as our new "light body," and carry on interactions with our brethren in this new way.

BETH:

So, you aren't sad when anyone physically dies and transitions into their "light body?"

MARTHA:

Absolutely not. It is a most joyous occasion! We celebrate such a transition with pride in ushering another spirit into the next vibrational level upward. It is not unlike the pride you feel upon graduation day at your schools.

Once we become non-physical, it also means we have a new mode of travel available to us. While physical, we can travel via a physical spacecraft to other locations or project an energetic version of ourselves. Once we become non-physical, we are able to travel through the use of what can be referred to as "angelic transport." I will explain what such angels are in a later conversation.

BETH:

I can't wait. You must feel my pile of questions forming. But by the sounds of it, maybe you can visit me here? So, I can see you "in person" through your energetic projection?

MARTHA:

That answer is still a "no," I'm afraid. Our vibration has reached a point that it is so high above your physical reality that neither my energetic nor physical form would be visible to your bodily eyes. For now, you can only see me within your mind, via your "inner eyes," which is a higher vibration than physical sight. This dialogue is about bringing your species closer to us and the type of reality we are living in, so that you may join us up here rather than we join you down there.

BETH:

Yes, I can "see" you quite clearly when we speak, but only if I focus on intending to do that.

MARTHA:

That is because the power of your thought directs your inner eyes to me. Think of my face or body and you can see me. Direct your thoughts elsewhere and away I go. The mind is very powerful, and few on your planet understand it. There are some texts that teach how this power can be used consciously. You yourself have a beginning understanding.

BETH:

Yes, not too long ago I wrote a short article about it. Is there a chance you would be interested in teaching us more about becoming a *conscious creator*? As you said, I have a beginning understanding, and would love to deepen what I know.

MARTHA:

Absolutely. Let us discuss further what it means to become a conscious creator.

CHAPTER 12

Becoming a Conscious Creator

MARTHA:

The first thing you must understand about how conscious creation works, is that your thoughts are creating all the time, whether you are aware of it or not. What makes the creation of your thoughts conscious, is that you are fully aware of the impact your thoughts are having on what you experience. You control the impact, not through controlling your thoughts, but rather, your beliefs.

It is when you truly believe the truths you read and hear that your thoughts about such things become powerful engines behind what you create and therefore manifest in the physical world. There is no room for mindless repetition of "magical" phrases or an intense struggle to find "happy thoughts" that you do not truly feel. A world will rise in response to true and honest feelings, regardless of whether they are positive or negative. What you must do then, is actively seek out those thoughts you do not want, and consciously change your mind about them. This requires great willingness and strong vigilance at the outset, but once you begin to experience the happy results of rightminded thinking, you will never cease in it. Those truths you once tried to apply to your life through mindless repetition will suddenly become the mindful fabric of your whole reality. You will begin to manifest truth. You will witness what your world sees as "miraculous occurrences." Life will indeed become quite otherworldly as compared with those around you. All this stems from a simple shift in what you truly believe, and you will know if your beliefs have shifted, through the peace that you feel. Feelings are the voice of what you believe. Thoughts are the engine upon which your beliefs ride, which are carried to your heart where you feel them.

Thought, belief and feelings are intricately connected to

one another. Ultimately, you can judge where your beliefs rest through how you feel. Thoughts one way or the other are irrelevant unless they produce a feeling in you through belief in them. Making statements or thinking thoughts you do not truly believe produce no emotionally charged feeling, which results in non-creative forces.

This is why mindless repetition of affirmations or your "Law of Attraction" produce erratic results. The problem lies not in the positive phrases themselves, as many do align quite perfectly with the truth about you. However, this alignment is only half of the power behind the ideas. The other half stems from your belief as to whether such thoughts are true for you or not. The results become erratic because only some people truly believe such affirmations and only some of the time. When used without belief, such words become meaningless. All beliefs create one of two things: they are either creating what is eternally true with God or making what is false and out of alignment with God's Love for you. These are thoughts you think alone, with your ego. If your beliefs align with the truth as God knows it to be for you, then the power of the universe is at your disposal.

There is yet another caveat. You cannot manifest joy if what you are trying to manifest is not in alignment with eternal joy. Let me state this again in another way. You cannot manifest love if what you are trying to manifest is not in alignment with eternal love. And again, you cannot manifest abundance if what you are trying to manifest is not in alignment with eternal abundance. I will state this one more time, just to be as clear as possible. You cannot manifest the truth of anything in life if what you are trying to manifest is not in alignment with the truth of eternal life.

Do you see the important qualifying factor in all that you want to manifest? Your thoughts about what you desire to manifest must be in alignment with eternal beliefs, or your mind is not in alignment with God's. If you are out of alignment with God's Mind, what you manifest will be of your mind alone, or the ego, and you will not be happy with your experience.

It is a misunderstanding that God does not want you to have

abundance here in this reality of physical form, time and space. God wants you to feel abundant, loved and happy wherever you think you are. However, He can only give you what you ask for. And if you ask for what is not eternal, then you will be gravely disappointed every single time. Only what is eternal is real, because only what is real will last for all eternity.

If you align your thoughts with what is eternal, then you will be given a real experience containing eternal joy.

BETH:

How is this done? How do you align your thoughts with God's eternal Mind?

MARTHA:

You must use your intellectual understanding to convert thoughts into beliefs which ignite your power to truly create.

Take this supreme truth for example: God has given all power unto you to create.

Though you can understand these words intellectually, the idea is abstract, and most have a difficult time truly believing them. So how does one come to believe words that do not seem applicable to them?

Begin first by asking yourself, "Do I feel these words in my heart? Can I truly feel the quiet strength of the power, joy and sense of deep security that comes from belief in them?" If so, joy, emotional security and total trust will have replaced all other feelings of "inner struggle."

Most likely you will feel just the opposite. You will feel unworthy of such power.

BETH:

So, how do you realize this power?

MARTHA:

Most people want many things in life; all the things they think will bring them the happiness they seek, such as money, a life partner, health, a profitable job, and so on and so forth.

And yet, why do you want any of these things to begin with? What is it these things seem to bring you? They seem to bring you joy, emotional security and control over your life.

However, such worldly things elicit happiness in you, not because of what they are, but because of how they make you feel. And yet, once such things are attained, the joy of having them quickly fades and you begin your search for joy anew. And so, it seems, you are unhappy whether you have or do not have such things, situations and relationships as you desire from this world. Why is this? It is because such things are not rooted in eternal beliefs which is where truth springs forth into the world to manifest God's Reality instead of the one you are each currently manifesting.

Now I am going to explain to you how to take your first baby steps towards attaining monumental eternal beliefs aligned with the creative force of God Himself and thus bring about a new reality—Heaven on Earth.

What if I told you that the true order of creating is that you must be happy first before anything in your outer life can make a shift?

You might feel some resistance to this statement. You may insist that you genuinely need external things to change first, before you can truly feel happy. You may insist that these external factors are the cause of your feelings of dis-ease and therefore must be dealt with, corrected and changed before you can shift out of your negative, fear-based feelings.

And I am going to tell you, it is the other way around. It is not the person, place or thing that must change, but rather, the feeling you have assigned to the idea of having or not having it.

Now let us come back to the idea that God has given all power unto you. You want to believe this, but do not yet feel it as joyous truth in your heart. You have not assigned your happiness to this concept, yet deep down, this is what you are really after. This is what you truly want: to know your divine power to create—to "know thyself," and you search the world over, assigning that feeling to various people, places and things you have decided will bring you joy and security.

BETH:

So how do you move from assigning your greatest joy from the external to the internal? How do you feel happiness and ease within your being first, before anything external changes?

MARTHA:

It is a gentle process of moving from thought into belief. This need not take a long time, just careful consideration to allow your mind to adjust to foreign concepts such as, "God has given all power unto you to create." Merely accept these words as true and such will be your experience. Yet to get there, you must experience the results of such belief.

Herein lies what appears to be a paradox that sounds almost impossible to overcome. This is why it has been called a miracle once it has been achieved.

In order to attain a belief before you experience proof that it is the truth, you must believe first and see after.

The ego says, "Seeing is believing." The Voice of the Holy Spirit within you says, "Believing is seeing."

It is truly a miracle to reverse your thinking in this way. The world you currently see is the complete opposite of the way things are in the eternal realities and in order to experience the abundance that surrounds you now, you must believe first and ask questions later.

Your beliefs must arrive at this fundamental truth: the power of God runs through all creation, sustaining all living and non-living things, adhering them together as one Unified Whole. And each of you is an essential part of that Whole.

You see what you want because of what you believe. If you change what you believe, you will see the truth instead. You will see, know, feel and experience your oneness with all creation. It is this power behind all things that you must come to believe is real, and only this is true.

BETH:

What is this power?

MARTHA:

It is the Love of God. Currently, you are simply molding it into what you want. Change your beliefs and you will change your whole reality.

Now, back to how to shift your thoughts into alignment with eternal beliefs in order to align your mind with the Mind of God so that what you manifest brings you nothing but eternal joy.

All you must do is remember the power of God that lies behind all that you see in your physical world and know that this, and only this, is the truth about your reality. All else is false. It is a cover behind which you hide the glory and light that you truly are.

Before you react to anything, ask yourself if you have first looked for the light behind what you see. If you do not feel peace, you have not found the light and therefore do not believe in it. If you want to become the powerful creator that you are in truth, you must come to believe in the light within all things.

Most of the time, you seem to give little attention to your thoughts and so they carry your feelings all over the place at any given moment. Your creative power lacks focus and direction, and so your life seems to unfold without focus or direction, which causes great distress and anxiety.

Most often, you do not like what you feel, and so you receive more of what you do not want—and you do not know you are simply reflecting your inner self.

Do you want to become a conscious creator?

Then first, begin with your thoughts. Start small. Focus on something you find pleasant, such as the feel of your heartbeat, air moving through your lungs, petting the cat or dog, or just let your eyes rest on something lovely.

The second step is to slowly turn your thoughts inward. Notice the love you feel. Love is the vibration you extend to the world in order that it be reflected back to you. What you give, you will receive. This is your God-given power to create. Love is the language of God.

The third step is to continue to wean yourself off the external thing you are focusing on and move inward even deeper. Realize, the thing itself does not bring you joy, but the Eternal Power within ALL things. Let your mind expand beyond this world of time and form and into the realm of the eternal. Feel the interconnectedness you have with all Creation.

Fourth, you will then begin to feel your power, as you expand from your physical ego-self and reach for your eternal Oneself, Who is unified with All Creation.

For most, this state will last but a few moments before old fear-based thoughts creep back in. Do not let this deter you, for as you practice allowing your thoughts to align with Love, you will find that it builds momentum. Positive things will begin to synchronize in your life, as your positive thoughts align your feelings with the vibration of your Creator; the vibration of Love.

As I stated previously, this does not mean you can never have a negative thought ever again, for fear the world will come crumbling down around you. Never forget there is great power in "catching yourself" in such thoughts and remembering that you do not want them. It is your very recognition of them that brings about transformation. Do not try to force them away or keep them buried, for this will only make them stronger. Resistance begets only suffering. Simply notice your feelings and use your power of decision to shift your focus onto even the smallest loving thought. It is through your decision to love that transforms the pain. Through love, you align your thoughts with the Power that unites us all together. God will then take the next step, closing the gap between thought and belief, and you will experience the feeling of joyful expansion and the security of your Oneself. Nothing else will ever satisfy you. This is what you search the whole world over for. Belief comes from consciously extending God's Love and experiencing His Love reflected back to you. Herein lies your power to consciously create, even as God does.

One of the most important things for you to learn about becoming a conscious creator is this: your attraction to God's Eternal Unifying Love is the highest expression there is of the "Law of Attraction." Once you become attracted to this and this alone, you will find everything.

BETH:

That was beautiful and extremely helpful to me Martha. Thank you. I feel the need to share a quote from *A Course in Miracles* here, as what you've just taught reminds me of it so much.

"Few appreciate the real power of the mind, and no one remains fully aware of it all the time.... The mind is very powerful, and never loses its creative force. It never sleeps. Every instant it is creating. It is hard to recognize that thought and belief combine into a power surge that can literally move mountains. It appears at first glance that to believe such power about yourself is arrogant, but that is not the real reason you do not believe it. You prefer to believe that your thoughts cannot exert real influence because you are actually afraid of them... There are no idle thoughts. All thinking produces form at some level."

A Course in Miracles Text 2.VI.9:3

CHAPTER 13

Attaining Miracle Mindedness

BETH:

I think I understand the idea behind becoming a conscious creator, but I would love some specific examples of how to turn around my day-to-day thoughts. It seems my mind is constantly focused on what I think I want in this world and I'd love a quick mental correction for these specific thoughts. What should I be thinking in order to realign myself with eternal thoughts so that I don't get off track? What exactly am I supposed to be thinking?

MARTHA:

Yes, I will most certainly go over such specifics with you. These things concern every human mind on the planet, and it is time to live aligned with eternally creative thoughts rather than the self-destructive thoughts of the ego.

I will begin by clarifying that as yet, most of you are not even aware which of your thoughts are self-destructive. You are largely content to dwell upon your desires, such as "love," money or some form of material abundance, and health. All that you want or need falls under one of these three categories in one way or another. What you do not realize, is that by focusing on these areas with a heart that does not know the truth of what you want—the truth behind the need to feel fulfilled by them—you are only going to manifest suffering. Let us address each of them as I explain the change of mind necessary that will bring about a new perspective which will shift your beliefs into alignment with Source.

We will begin with the idea of love. As you understand it, love is the emotional dedication of one person to another. It also involves bodily proximity for the most part, as you each yearn for the physical nearness of those whom you care about. All this is understandable and quite alright. What becomes misaligned with Source, is when such needs are perceived as being unmet and you suffer emotional pain as a result. Any form of emotional suffering is a sure sign you are misaligned with Source. So, where did your thoughts of love go wrong when you feel hurt and unloved? Your thoughts went wrong when you omitted your understanding of eternal love—the truth about what love really is. When you apply the truth to your understanding, your beliefs will shift, and you will heal.

The truth is, love cannot die, be withheld or dissolved. What you perceive as hurtful forms of love are false love, being based upon the body, which is in itself false, as it is not your true identity. If, when you perceive thoughts of abandonment, neglect, rejection and so forth, fear not! Remind yourself that what you perceive is false. Only bodies can and do, behave this way towards one another, but let your mind simply rest in the quiet knowing that such relationships dissolve when the body dissolves. What you truly desire is an unending eternal love. Then remind yourself that it is already given. You and another are forever and always together and should you so desire to experience their presence, you will have that at any time you wish once bodies no longer separate you.

If another has caused you great pain and you wish to heal it, know that it is healed already, and only Love exists between you and you will perceive only this Love when your bodies are no more. The idea is to live as though you believe this is true for you now.

And so, the small shift in thinking necessary for manifesting the experience of love in your life, healing all your current relationships and feeling content completely on your own is this: live as though you believe in the universal Love that is yours now. Wake each day with the happy expectation that you have no idea how new love will enter your life or how your current relationships will be healed. Open your mind to any and all possibilities. Do not set any limits through specific expectations. Such thoughts are not aligned with eternal love, which is boundless, all around you and within you at all times. Simply understand that it is your feelings of joy through understanding this truth that will bring such love into manifestation as your physical experience. This is miracle-minded thinking. This is stepping beyond the boundaries of what you think this world can give and allowing your truth to unfold in ways you never expected

Now let us see how this idea applies to money or physical abundance in the world in whatever form you desire it. From your point of view, the body has many needs: food, clothing, shelter and so on and so forth. In order to provide those needs, you must buy them and therefore have a great need for money as your source of security and continuity for the body. We will call all such physical needs your "abundance." However, you cannot manifest abundance if what you are trying to manifest is not in alignment with eternal abundance. What is eternal abundance? The knowing that such needs are non-existent whence the body is no more. In truth, you have no needs whatsoever. This is the truth of your abundance. The idea is, to live as though you believe this is true for you now.

And so, the small shift in thinking necessary to manifesting all forms of abundance in your life is this: Live as though you believe in the universal Abundance that is yours now. Wake each day with the happy expectation that you have no idea how such abundance will enter your life or how your current sense of lack will be healed. Open your mind to any and all possibilities. Do not set any limits through specific expectations. Such thoughts are not aligned with eternal abundance, which is boundless, all around you and within you at all times. Simply understand that it is your feelings of joy through understanding this truth that will bring such abundance into manifestation as your physical experience. This is miracle minded thinking. This is stepping beyond the boundaries of what you think this world can give and allowing your truth to unfold in ways you never expected.

Lastly, let us apply this shift in thinking to the body itself, to your health. Currently, health to you is the perfect functioning of the body, without pain, disease or absence of any parts. What you fail to understand is that the body is not eternal, and therefore any state of its existence is a false state, whether you believe it to be healthy or unhealthy. You are an eternal being of limitless love, light and comfort. It is impossible for you to be unhealthy, although your awareness of such health as you are in truth can be blocked from your memory. Such frailties of the body will disappear whence the body is no more. This is the truth of your health; you are eternally perfect and whole. The idea is, to live as though you believe this is true for you now.

And so, the small shift in thinking necessary for manifesting all forms of health in your life is this: live as though you believe in the universal Health that is yours now. Wake each day with the happy expectation that you have no idea how such health will enter your life or how your current sense of disease will be healed. Open your mind to any and all possibilities. Do not set any limits through specific expectations. Such thoughts are not aligned with eternal health, which is boundless, all around you and within you at all times. Simply understand that it is your feelings of joy through understanding this truth that will bring such health into manifestation as your physical experience. This is miracle minded thinking. This is stepping beyond the boundaries of what you think this world can give and allowing your truth to unfold in ways you never expected.

CHAPTER 14

Live Aligned With Source

BETH:

I feel like I have a firm understanding now of what it means to consciously create and how to apply miracle-minded thinking to my life, but now I would love it if you explained how can we learn to do this on the level of your people?

MARTHA:

We cannot hope to satisfy all that you wish to understand here, in this one dialogue. Remember what I said at the outset: our conversations here are but one small part of a greater masterpiece of information not yet fully revealed on your planet. There are many others who are working to usher in humanity's awakening, and each has their own contribution to make.

What I am about to explain to you is a process that, once understood takes practice, willingness and commitment. Explaining it all in one sitting would be like trying to explain how to fly one of your jet planes to a toddler who is only just learning to speak and walk.

So, I will do my best to satisfy your desire to further understand this process of conscious creation, while also remaining as brief and simplistic as possible.

First you must understand this: it took my people thousands of years to become masters of conscious creation and not without the assistance of many visiting celestial beings along the way. Each time our society showed readiness for the next evolutionary spiritual step, we would receive our next divine bestowal, or visitor. Earth has had its own such visits, but that is another topic we will discuss later.

As we have already stated, conscious creation requires mastery of your thoughts, which are linked directly to your feelings. It is through your feelings that vibrational frequency is generated.

You know from your own experience that thought without feeling is nothing. In other words, if you simply change your thought or attempt to "think positive" you do not automatically change the way you feel. This is why belief is so important. Belief is the glue that holds thought and feeling together; belief is what lends your thoughts and feelings their vibrational power. Thoughts alone do not create. Thoughts beget feelings, which are triggered by the beliefs you have placed in the thoughts. Thoughts you do not believe do not trigger a feeling, except perhaps one of disbelief, which of course does not create or manifest.

We have just reviewed the basic foundation for conscious creation.

Your question then is how do you create the world you want, as easily as my own people do now? How do you get to the point of "moving mountains?"

Here again, the answer to that lies in what you believe. If your beliefs are based upon what is not true, even the faintest wind will not concede to your thoughts.

Your thoughts must therefore undergo purification. Purification of your thoughts is merely the process of distilling them down to the absolute truth and nothing else. Therefore, all false beliefs you hold about yourself must be let go of—which also includes what you believe about others, for they are part of you. This is the beginning of the one-mindedness my people now enjoy. It is the beginning of the acceptance that all minds are joined in One Mind.

Let us take our own relationship for example. The catalyst to our meeting was your extending a thought to the universe: the intention to extend your love to whatever life may exist in the farthest reaches of space and time. You did this with the belief that it was actually happening. This caused you to feel love actually extending from your heart. Your thought combined with belief into a real feeling which manifested into a real experience. And here I am. A real connection you have made through your intentional desire. You consciously created a situation that manifested into our current relationship.

And this is only the beginning of what you can do!

Align your thoughts with our Creator and you can do anything. Your will joined with God's Will through the power of your loving thoughts is an unstoppable force of creation!

But, in the beginning stages the steps will appear small or imperceptible. There also may be a delay or gap between thought and creation because of your beliefs centering around how things must take time to come into existence. Do not look for outward changes until your inner changes have been accomplished. As previously stated, the inner shift must come first. Align with love, joy and other similar emotions and these vibrations will go out before you as messengers from God Himself, making way for peace. In fact, above all else, desire peace and harmony with all things, for peace is what you would make manifest. The real trick is not holding any judgments or expectations about what and how such peace comes to you. Judgment and expectations instantly block your highest good from your awareness.

In fact, this is the most important idea to be vigilant for: do not judge or expect how life should unfold! Let go. Get out of the way. Do not try to fly the jet plane yet. Start small, focus on what makes you happy, then turn inward with those thoughts. Before you can move mountains, you must first learn to move your own heart.

As you practice staying aligned with the loving peaceful thoughts of Source, you will find that your external environment becomes more malleable. Situations that seemed to be in a rigid stalemate, or appeared to have no way out for you, will suddenly become flexible and "moveable." Such malleability will manifest as happy coincidences and synchronicities in your life. This will happen because your external circumstances are coming into alignment with your new higher alignment or vibration with Source.

Alignment with Source feels like harmony. It is to be at peace with all things as they are now. You accomplish this state through understanding the truth of the state all things, your state of eternal union with All That Is.

BETH:

For humanity in general, what area is in greatest need of healing right now? What is most out of alignment in us that needs to be brought into peace?

MARTHA:

The definition of Who You Are. You are in conflict about your true nature—your true identity. You believe you are separate from everyone else. You believe you are mere bodies living an isolated existence away from Source or God.

You who believe you are separate and outside the Mind of God, who are you without Him? You would be nothing without your connection to Source, for God is the power that sustains you. You are part of God's Mind as part of His One Creation. And therefore, you share in His power to create.

BETH:

To create what?

MARTHA:

Not what, but with. You are being called to create with Love, in harmony and peace. And what you create is the beautiful, kind and good. You can transform the whole world with such power. I bid you to try it! Begin with your relationships.

Relationships are situations, for you are in a relationship with All Things. When you find yourself in a situation/relationship to anything or anyone in your environment, align with Love and watch how things unfold. Everything will always work out perfectly, harmoniously and peacefully with no effort at all. All you must do to align with the Love of Source, is see yourself as part of them and they, of you. And as you both join in the light of this truth—the truth of your oneness—you share in Its Loving Benevolence and peace. Being aligned with this, the highest vibration of love, is the loving union of shared being in Oneness, which is to be aligned with God. This is because He sees you as joined and knows your Oneness beyond belief. Thus, you join with truth. This joining is the recognition of Love, which is the miracle from which all miracles flow.

If you want to start each day correctly, begin with this thought:

*Today I want only my highest good, and I ask this through
the Voice of Peace within me.
In every relationship—in every situation—I make peace my
only goal.
And with this goal kept firm, I know that only good can
come to me.*

Then watch how life unfolds! You are now a co-creator with the Mind of God, of which you are a part.

However, do not specify for certain things or events. How can you, who sees so little, know what your highest good is? It is not always what you think, so cease to think alone. Align yourself with God and through such intentions aligned in peaceful union only miracles will come.

Again, this is simply a good place to start. I say "start," because it is only the beginning of all the good that will come from such perfect alignment. These are your beginning steps to learning how to fly the jet plane—as co-pilot; not Captain.

Therefore, purify your thoughts down to nothing but peace, which again is harmonious recognition of your inherent oneness with God and all others who share life with you. Then you will soon begin to consciously create as you apply this thinking to all situations and every person.

You will not yet move mountains, but you will move hearts, as your own heart begins to beat in time with Love. This small willingness, the tiniest of steps you will ever take—will be enough to set the rest into place.

Do not forget that you are in relationship with every situation; the very ground you walk upon and the people you meet as you go. In each relationship, in each situation, ask yourself, "Am I at peace here, in this relationship/situation?"

If you feel any form of conflict, the answer is "no." Then actively seek to correct your thoughts to bring yourself back into alignment. You needn't solve the problem itself, right that moment. In fact, if the momentum of your feelings is strong enough, it may well be impossible to do so. Remember: you cannot always change your feelings simply by changing your thoughts. When these times arise, simply focus on something else—something that truly does bring you peace. Use this as a focal point. Then you will at least cease to attack your own identity—your Oneness. For when you feel attack and conflict, you have indeed forgotten you are One.

When you truly believe in such Oneness, you act on it. This is how one undoes the effects of time and moves into eternity. This final phase is where my people are right now in our spiritual development.

BETH:

So, we still have thousands of years ahead of us?

MARTHA:

No. Here is the beautiful part: what I am speaking of here can be achieved in an instant. That is the paradox of time versus eternity. Moving from time into eternity takes no time at all—since eternity is beyond the realm of time. To move up from the vibration of time and physical matter you only need to achieve the proper thoughts, which you must come to believe, which then allow for the miraculous transition from your current reality up to the next.

Mountains do not move in your reality—the low vibration you live in now—but in mine. Believe you can rise to where I am and everything that does not vibrate at this frequency will fall away as your world falls into place—or rather, "rises" to the occasion.

And let it be clearly understood; the very fabric of physical existence, including the material that makes up an entire mountain, does not move, shift or change because we commanded it to do so. It is because our minds are in total union with the truth—that we are at one with every aspect of creation, limitless in our power and our peace—that material existence responds. It is our belief in this truth that unites us with the very fabric of our physical world, and in response to our vibration of love, the world cannot help but join our will with it and become whatever it is we need it to be. Love is the most powerful creative force there is—and the only creative force. It is not coercive, and neither does it command, but merely is and what love touches cannot help but become what you will—out of love for you in return.

BETH:

Oh, I love that! Thank you for expanding on this idea.

One last small thing and this may be a bit off the subject: People will ask me why you use the male pronoun "Him" when referring to God. Please explain that.

MARTHA:

I do this only because it is the most comfortable vernacular for you, as you write. If your society were based upon a matriarch, I would use "Her." Know this: our Creator is All That Is and therefore All Inclusive. This includes all manifestations of gender. Our Creator is beyond all form or gender, but for ease of your writing we will refer to Him using the male pronoun. Let it be understood that no female exclusion is intended by either of us.

CHAPTER 15

How An Evolved Society Is Arranged

BETH:

Speaking of gender, how is your society arranged? What are your relationships like? Do you make love as we do? Do you have gender roles?

MARTHA:

All of these questions can be answered in the same way: We are one. We are one in awareness and mind. Therefore, we truly understand that what we do to another, we do to ourselves. There is no need for government; we immediately know what our needs are, and how best to cooperate to solve such problems as they arise. No one from "outside" need direct our actions. This may sound like a "hive" mentality, but we each maintain our own individual personalities and choices. We have learned that the best choice is always the most loving one.

Because we are all connected through the mind and can easily share experiences, in a sense we are all living multiple lives all at once. Therefore, we have no need for repeat journeys to this world once we are finished with our physical form here. We have one incarnation in this bodily form and can live for what would be counted as hundreds and sometimes several thousand of your earth years.

BETH:

If you live for hundreds of years, doesn't your planet risk overpopulation?

MARTHA:

No. First, because as a general rule, we only procreate once per lifetime per couple and some of us volunteer not to procreate at all. And second, because again, we are only semi-physical. Not all of us are here on the planet in the physical all the time. And some of us have collaborated with other beings from other dimensions of time and space and have traveled with them to far off places in physical form via spaceships, a situation which is in constant flux. So, our population is quite sustainable and self-regulated. Not to mention we live in what you would think of as a "natural state," in complete harmony with the balance of nature, as part of nature. We self-regulate our population so as to not overwhelm our environment. We also have the option to live anywhere on the planet; either sea or land. This dual adaptation opens up vast amounts of physical space for living options.

Now, back to how our society is arranged. We first form into small family groups consisting of mother, father and children. We have already discussed how many children we have and how often we procreate. As for sex, yes, we will couple to fertilize our eggs but once in a lifetime. That does not mean we do not make love. This type of union happens on the energetic plane where we are non-physical. What you consider physical lovemaking is not actually making love. Love is a joining as one, and bodies, despite how close you can be to one another, even to the point of physical coupling, is still not making love. It is merely the bringing of bodies together for physical pleasure, which can be done with either loving or unloving intentions. Either way, it is not actually lovemaking. Love is joining and only minds can truly join.

Therefore, a true state of making love is the experience of union or oneness with another and such union cannot be achieved with bodies. Our lovemaking is therefore on the energetic level and far exceeds any physical experience even the most proficient lovemaker on your world has ever had. It would in fact, quite literally "blow your mind" if any of us should unleash the full power of our love upon you. It would instantly remove you from your body and you would never want to return, the density of it being too much to bear after such an experience.

So, do not be disappointed to hear that physical sex or what you call "making love" will eventually evolve into use only for procreation. What it becomes is something I scarce can find words in your language to describe.

After the family unit, society gathers into small groups of individuals formed around those who were born together and are thus of the same age. Such groups become what you could call a "town" and thereby arrange themselves for optimal living. We may find our partner within our own cluster or we can move to another, if we so choose. We partner for life. There is no separation or "divorce" in that all unions are based on a relationship of love—or what you understand to be a "holy relationship." No one is excluded from the collective love of the society, so there is no need to look elsewhere for another partner. All love is given equally to all.

BETH:

So, is there any romance?

MARTHA:

You mean "special" love? No. Not as you believe you need it. There is no reason to hold anyone else above another as we are all collectively loving towards each other. In this sense, we cannot "cheat" on our partner—it benefits everyone if love is shared among us. Again, no one leaves their partner, because to look for another would be to find what they already have. It might please you to know however, that those with whom you struggle now, in your holy and un-holy love relationships, remain with you throughout your incarnations. Your evolving relationships are bringing you to the place where we are now—believe it or not. And these same souls you now travel with will be the ones who will still be with you as time goes on, and you will one day couple with them in spirit in the way we do now.

As for gender roles, yes, we have male and female bodies, but aside from the males carrying the sperm for fertilization and females the eggs, there is no real physical difference between us. Therefore, we have no special roles assigned to gender specific duties. Men and women are complete equals in our society.

Do not get the impression that we do not "fall in love." The love we feel is not a "fall" in vibration at all, but a rise. The intensity of what we feel for one another is unrivaled in your world.

BETH:

Got it, thank you for your wonderful and complete answer. Now for my next question: what is your religion like? Do you have a religion?

MARTHA:

We have no organized institutionalized religion as your world understands it. Religion is purely personal between God and the individual—it is beyond our comprehension how it could ever be made into a structured institution.

Each individual is clearly guided from within by our Creator, Who's Voice can be plainly heard. There is no need for outside guidance. We are each guided through that which comes from Source Itself.

BETH:

Okay, I figured as much, given how spiritually evolved your people are. Next question: what do your people do for a living? What are some of the jobs or work that goes on in your society?

MARTHA:

We do not work to earn money, as you do on your world. There is no need for such exchange. Our homes are crafted out of the terrain itself through the simple power of our thoughts and our food comes from what we cultivate on land or sieve from the sea. No one need "buy" anything. It is all readily available. Neither is there disease, famine or any form of "crime." All of these things have come into balance as our minds have come into alignment with our Source and Center, whom you call God. All problems as you see them now on your planet have disappeared on ours. Our society has become healed and whole because our minds have become healed and whole.

BETH:

What do you do all day long then?

MARTHA:

Once the mind is healed, there is no need to toil or strive for anything in any way. This frees up enormous amounts of time to pursue the desires of the heart. Life becomes a thing of constant joy and beauty as each of us takes on those tasks we enjoy most. Some of us are drawn to such things as the pursuit of cultivating plants and enhancing our food supply—but keep in mind, this is not seen as "work." Such work is done with the joy of your most enthusiastic botanists. As stated before, we also enjoy composing music, while others explore worlds and realms beyond our own, and some love to teach love, as I am doing now, here with you. My greatest joy is teaching others about the path to Love's awareness. Besides what I have briefly mentioned here, there are many other vocations, callings and activities that we do in our day-to-day life but would be beyond explanation or compare with what you have in your current reality.

BETH:

So, you don't get paid in any way for your work? You just do things for the fun of it?

MARTHA:

Look at what you are doing now, as you sit here typing our conversation. Are you getting paid to do this work?

BETH:

No.

MARTHA:

Then why are you doing it?

BETH:

Because it's exciting! There's nothing else I'd rather be spending my free time doing.

MARTHA:

Then there you have your answer. Our "work" is whatever our greatest excitement is. And we love every second of it. No further compensation in order to feel fulfilled is necessary.

Also, I wish to alleviate the impression that as beings evolve into the non-physical that all activity ceases to be. This idea could not be farther from the truth. You will have more abilities, more interests and more joyful experiences than you can currently comprehend once you embark on your full-fledged eternal journey.

BETH:

Yes, I think many of us fear "the collective mind" or becoming one with "All That Is" because we think we'll disappear into a diaphanous cloud and cease to exist or sit on an actual cloud playing the harp all day. Boring! We really have no idea what to expect, and so we generally fear such a transition.

MARTHA:

Nothing could be further from the truth. To be "at one" with all creation does not mean you must then give up your individual awareness of your personality. What would be the point of your existence if you were created only to be reintegrated with Totality and eventually "erased?" Such a thing shall never come to pass. Your light, love and your particular personal perspective and awareness will never be extinguished. You are "you" and will forever be you, for all eternity but you will also one day become aware of your wholeness with your Creator and all that is created— from your own unique perspective and personality.

This is how our Creator experiences life—by living through your awareness of all that is, through union with you. You could say you are the drop of water in the ocean, but rather than dis- solving into it and disappearing, you retain the ability to know you are a drop. I assure you, one day you will know yourself as both the drop and the ocean. A most wondrous place of awareness indeed.

Until then, fear not! You have real business to get done, but you will not view it as work as you do now in your present reality. It will be an undertaking of love that will never cease to amaze you. You have worlds upon worlds to discover and enjoy, as well as bring your knowledge and experiences to. The universe and your Creator eagerly await your integration with All That Is. You will not lose yourself in it, but rather, find your Self.

CHAPTER 16

Planet Neba

BETH:

I can't believe I haven't asked you this question yet! What do you call yourselves? And what is the name of your planet?

MARTHA:

The closest translation to what we call ourselves in your language would be "The People of Song."

BETH:

Okay, that makes sense, given your unique talents for singing.

MARTHA:

As for the name of our planet, it is called Neba (pronounced: neb-bah). This name is a shortened version of the name Nebadon, in honor of our (and your) local universe.

BETH:

What do you mean by "local universe?"

MARTHA:

Your planet is located on the edge of the local universe called Nebadon, which is on the edge of superuniverse 7, which is called Orvonton. And here I must reveal to anyone unfamiliar with this knowledge, that your world is not actually called "earth" by those of us living in the higher, spiritual dimensions of the superuniverse. It is referred to as "Urantia" in the upper, less-dense physical realities, of which my world is a part. In fact, there are many names for your planet, another common one being, Terra.

BETH:

This sounds like material from The Urantia Book.

MARTHA:

It most certainly can be found there, as well as much of what we are about to discuss in the forthcoming chapters. We are about to embark on a series of conversations that contain information that will open and challenge the minds of many.

There are two directions we can go from here: we can talk about the physical worlds of space and time, or the eternal worlds where no physical body can go. Since my people are in transition as semi-physical, we have knowledge of both, as we are learning to ascend from the worlds of physical space and time to the eternal. Which would you like to begin with?

BETH:

Let's start with the physical worlds of space and time, then move into the eternal realms. It seems logical to move "upward" in that way so to speak.

MARTHA:

Excellent! I will keep things as simple and brief as possible. Some of this information can be overwhelming, so I will give only a cursory overview where I can. I will begin by explaining how the superuniverses are arranged.

Your planet is one of many inhabited worlds, which comprise what is known as a "local universe" which, we have already established, is called Nebadon.

Your universe, combined with many other similar universes in size and arrangement, make up what is called a superuniverse which is named Orvonton.

Your superuniverse has a capital called Uversa. And it is from Uversa that the celestial beings that communicated The Urantia Book came.

Yours is one of seven such superuniverses, and we are all on a never-ending, never-beginning circle of spiritual evolution of time and eternity together within the larger "body" of God—our Creator and Source Who holds us in existence within His Loving Embrace. God is our Source and Center from Whom All Creation starts and issues therefrom.

The seven superuniverses combined are called The Multiverse or Grand Universe.

Within each superuniverse, there are around one trillion inhabitable planets. The farther out from the center you go, the fewer and more spread out the systems. The farther inward you go, the closer together and more clustered the systems become. Each planet has its own assigned number and name. Your planet, Urantia, is number 606. We are not certain of the exact number of inhabited worlds, in that new life is constantly in the process of coming into physical existence, while other worlds are transitioning into the eternal realms. Only our Universal Father knows all locations and numbers of the inhabited planets of space and time.

At the very center of creation—in the very Heart of God—lies a place called Havona and within Havona is a place called the Isle of Paradise, which is the central dwelling place of our eternal Creator. This is the central point from which all things radiate outward as extensions of God's Love. All seven superuniverses extend outward like three dimensional spokes of a wheel—think of a sphere if you will, or the slices of an orange—from our Source and Center. And as you travel inwardly through vibrational elevation, you pass through seven different concentric circles of density or new realities. The lowest vibrational reality is at the seventh or outermost ring; that of physical time and space, which you are currently experiencing. The rings of reality move in descending order from seven to one as you travel inward. For example, from where you are now in the seventh ring, you will eventually graduate inward to the sixth ring, where the eternal realities begin until you reach the innermost sanctum—the Heart of God, or what you could call "ground zero."

The other six eternal realities are not governed by the laws of physical time and space such as exist in the seventh outer ring. The seventh ring was invented or "made" by you and all of us, the creations of God, who decided to experience a place where God was not. And so, through our conscious choice to experience separation, the energy of our intention birthed the physical worlds of time and space—which is an experience of everything that is in complete opposition to the truth of our eternal unified identity as our Source created us to be.

Why we did this, will be answered in a later discussion.

Let it be understood at this point, that Heaven then, is not an actual place, but a state of existence also located within each of us, as we are each contained within God, and He is within us. And within God—at His Center—lies what you can refer to as Heaven. And so it is, we each carry Heaven within us. It is not a physical reality, but an experience of existence.

Understand clearly, you cannot get there by spaceship or any external means. It is an inward journey—a spiritual ascension. Ceasing to choose to come to the worlds of physical reality that lie in the seventh outermost ring of all creation is just one small step in getting there—one small step in the decision to stop seeking outside yourselves in the world of physical time and space for fulfillment. You are each here in a body to essentially make the choice to change directions from seeking outward to seeking inward for the truth. The reality you are currently experiencing is on the bottom rung of the energetic ladder inward and upward in vibration towards Havona.

There are different realities in what could also be referred to as other dimensions or frequencies or energetic vibrations—however you want to think of it. Currently, you are experiencing a state of being in the lowest and most limited vibration: that of physical form in the realm of time and space. It is a state that every single one of you chose to experience, but it is not your true state of being. Physical form is a state you made yourself, out of the desire to experience limitation or what could be called "separation from Source." Once you choose to remember your Union with Source and cease to feel the need to return to this limited level of self-expression, you will remember your eternal Oneself, of which I am a part, as well as untold hosts of other eternal beings. Again, your physical form is not who you are and the physical reality you are immersed in is not your true home. This is why every single one of you feels as though you do not belong, and you search for ways to "be someone." You are an expansive, magnificent, eternal personality, but you cannot know this until you decide to give up your belief in being something limited. Only your eternal self is real.

As you climb the "vibrational ladder" so-to-speak, your perception of reality will also shift. It will shift to include a great variety of spiritual beings, and life on other worlds that exist beyond your current and very limited physical vision. You will join the awakened creations in light and life as you progress in your individual spiritual development. And know that your personal development cannot be impeded by the overall progress of your society. Everyone must make his or her own journey; no one can do this for you, but neither can you be held back by the mass consciousness of your planet.

What lies beyond your current reality is beyond your wildest imaginations.

The eternal worlds all recognize and worship the Universal Father, Who created only what is like unto Himself—He therefore only created what is eternal and infinite. All else that exists as finite in physical form in the realm of time and space, is considered "unreal" in that it is a vibrational dimension made by the will of the created alone—meaning all of us who desired to experience "separation from Source." We are the self-willed creatures who have chosen to forget our eternal Source and our own eternal Self and have now embarked upon the long journey Home. We are on the adventure of attaining our memory of God the Father. The transcendent goal of we, the children of time, is to rediscover our eternal Creator and to comprehend our divine nature, and thereby recognize the Universal Source.

The forgetting of Who You Are is the metaphorical "deep sleep of Adam." My people are presently awakening and in the process of transition back into the state of permanent eternal form, and our world is being transformed along with us. It is my goal to help your people make great advancement towards this goal as well.

That being said, the seven superuniverses are very active. New systems and planets are constantly evolving, while others are passing away from material existence into the eternal realms.

You may feel you have been largely left to your own devices on your planet, alone and driftless in the cosmic sea of the unknown. But there are a multitude of Personalities or beings in charge of every single energy function that exists.

There is, operating throughout the vast realms and inhabited worlds of time and space, an intelligent control behind everything; for both the physical and non-physical spiritual. For example, there are beings called Gravity Presences that are continually exerting their majestic power of force in perfect harmony to keep your planet spinning as it is. You may have known about gravity for a long time, but what you did not know was that it is a real and living "presence." It does not have a personality or awareness in the way you understand it, but it is indeed alive.

CHAPTER 17

Beings On Other Worlds

BETH:

So, what are the other beings like out there, living on other inhabited worlds?

MARTHA:

As far as life on other planets goes, it is as mixed and varied as that of your own world, and then some. As far as upright, bipedal humanoid beings such as yourself goes, there are seven types living in the realm of physical time and space. That being said, as all types of beings spiritually ascend, we will eventually converge together on the higher levels of existence looking much the same. When that time comes, material differences between us as planetary beings will be of no more significance than the differences you perceive between yourselves on Urantia.

To support life in the manner you enjoy, planetary conditions must be within a certain range of sunlight, size and temperature to sustain advanced life forms. This much your scientists know. Therefore, there is nothing too strange or extreme by way of living standards between the bipedal beings, as far as that is concerned.

All planets are gradual in development when it comes to evolving life. This process is the same for every living species on every planet—and it is intentional. It may not be predictable, but it is not accidental.

All planets begin to harbor living organisms by the decree of the Life Carriers who decide when a planet is ready for their implantation. Life Carriers are an order of eternal celestial being, who's function it is to do exactly that which their name implies: carry life from system to system, spreading it intentionally across the seventh ring of physical time and space reality. They are the living catalysts who ignite material life; they mobilize matter through infusing it with the living energy of our Creator Father. Though the ways such life manifests after the initial implantation by the Life Carriers may vary greatly, it always begins in the same way: with a single protoplasmic cell that suddenly "comes to life" as its circuits are energized with the living light and love of our Source and Center through the infusion from a Life Carrier.

Aside from initial similarities, no two worlds are exactly alike, each planet having its own scale and diversity in living organisms. Everything evolves, but due to differences in living conditions, what manifests can vary greatly from planet to planet.

All planetary evolution proceeds from the same beginning. First comes the vegetation, then the animal life. The development of lower organisms happens first, and then higher forms proceed from there. This is not accidental. An orderly process is followed by the Life Carriers, who pre-determine what type of life modifications each planet will contain.

As I stated, there are seven types of bipedal physical beings, but there are thousands of sub-types and variants of these seven. The basic variations are:

1. Beings that breathe air. Your atmosphere on Urantia is ideal for supporting the breathing type of being.

2. Beings who have adapted to life in an ecosystem other than land. On some worlds, the highest order of being adapts to the water or the air much as you have adapted to the land. All this depends, of course, on planetary conditions. For instance, my people are an example of those who have adapted first to water. This is not too difficult to imagine. Had evolution taken a different turn, your people could have evolved from birds, and been air or a flying-type of creature. Had you evolved along the lines of whales and seals you could have been air breathers who lived primarily under water.

3. Land beings distinctly shaped by the gravity of their planet. Physical size is determined by the gravity of the planet we live on. The average mortal in Nebadon is roughly just less than seven feet tall. Some are as small as only two

feet, while the tallest are upwards of tens of feet. In your system, there is only one planet with people below four feet tall.

4. Beings who live at a temperature outside what you would call "normal." Beings can evolve to withstand a wide variety of temperatures. You are considered to be mid-temperature beings in your system.

5. Beings who utilize energy directly from their environment, converting it into electricity. All beings adapt and react to sunlight and other outside energies coming in through their planet's atmosphere slightly different. Some beings can actually convert the energy from their sun into electrical energy—recharging their bodies much as you would recharge a battery.

6. Beings who use photosynthesis for energy. Just as you take in oxygen and perform a gas exchange in your lungs in order to sustain your bodies, other life forms vary on how this is done. Some are completely non-breathers who take in energy directly from sunlight, much as your plants use photosynthesis.

7. There are a few additional types of beings in existence with unique variations that do not fall into any of the above categories. Such differences are difficult to explain to you, in that you have no point of reference from which to compare or understand them. These differences between you are purely anatomical and in no way impede that being's ability to evolve intellectually or spiritually as you do. Though they may look and function quite differently, they have a soul-personality just the same as you and me.

All types listed above are represented in your system, but some are quite rare. Despite these variations, understand that we are each relatable and recognizable to one another if or when we should come into contact, while still in our physical forms. This is done through telepathic means, or "soul recognition." Evolved beings simply recognize the "mark of God" in one another.

Another feature worth noting, is that most intelligent beings give single, live births with multiple births at once being the exception rather than the norm. My people are among the exception to this general evolutionary rule in that as I explained earlier, we gestate our young in semi-soft eggs, usually two to four at a time. At the time of hatching, the mother will birth the eggs either on land or in water as our young can breathe in either environment immediately. We typically choose to allow our young to hatch in the sea or in a vat of water on land, as it is the most natural transition from their egg. They arrive in the world already able to communicate telepathically and are fully capable of moving and feeding independently. They physically reach adulthood by the age of four of your Urantia years.

Knowing these variations are out there and the high degree to which intelligent life exists, it may worry some of you that a race of beings may one day visit you and take over your world in a hostile manner.

I would like to assure you that measures are currently in place to ensure that will never happen. On all other normal planets—planets that did not default into rebellion as yours did—the technological development never gets ahead of the spiritual development. Those planets that have the technology to reach you also possess matching spiritual advancement in light and love. They have advanced far beyond your primitive and aggressive behavior towards one another.

Those planets that have evolved technologically, but are spiritually regressed, and are considered "dangerous" are closely watched by the peaceful beings of higher realms. Those that have contacted Urantia and are currently, or have in the past, manipulated humanity in a negative way, are about to be shifted out of your reality. Or rather, humanity is about to shift to a higher dimension, out of their reach. You have the power to do this on an individual scale if ever confronted with a negative entity of any kind, shape or form, from any existence. All you must simply do, is move from a state of fear, to one of love and you shift out of reach from the lower vibrations. Extend your "enemies" love, and you not only heal yourself of fear, but you heal them as well.

Through extending love, you cancel out fear and your "enemy" will often simply disappear before your very eyes.

Therefore, you are effectively safe from any potentially hostile beings in the superuniverse permanently taking over your planet. Tyranny of any world over another does not last, for as a race evolves, their reality moves out of reach from such dark energies.

All beings on all worlds eventually become peacefully social. This is because it must be learned that we can only advance through cooperation and working together in peaceful union. It is through our relationships to one another that we advance both physically and spiritually.

We all share the same ways of thinking, having been endowed with the same Mind from the Infinite Spirit. All of us are literally "kindred spirits," despite any physical differences. And when we die, we all go through the same process and arrive at the same destination in the eternal realms after physical death. We are all on the same progressive spiritual path. And along the way, we all enjoy the same assistance, love and guidance of our guardian angels and other divine helpers. We also all share the same Christ Michael and God the Father of our creation.

In other words, despite our physical difference we are each more alike than we are different.

Take great care to bear these thoughts in mind when the time comes for you to physically encounter such a being from another world on your planet.

CHAPTER 18

Christ Michael

MARTHA:

The most startling thing about your planet is that, among some one trillion inhabited worlds in our superuniverse, Urantia was the planet chosen by Christ Michael for his one required human incarnation.

A Master Spirit is assigned to care for and assist each one of the seven superuniverses. Christ Michael is the name of our superuniverse Master Spirit.

In order for a Master Spirit to claim true sovereignty over His superuniverse, he must incarnate as one of each type of his creations in order that he may fully understand each creature's experience firsthand. There is no other way to acquire the viewpoint of the creature, than to temporarily become one of them. It is only then that a Creator Son can say they truly know and understand their creations.

Each incarnation is called a "bestowal" and there are seven types of creature bestowals a Creator Son must experience, including that of the order of angel and several other types of celestial being. Mortal time-bound bodies are the only truly physical or "form based" incarnation in existence. All other creature creations are from the non-physical or eternal realms. Again, each of the Seven Master Spirits is required to do this once for each of His seven orders of created beings for all eternity.

Christ Michael completed his one bestowal incarnation as a mortal on Urantia as the man you know as Jesus.

Because of the violent and dramatic way he exited his material experience on Urantia, your planet is renowned throughout the superuniverse as the "planet of the cross."

BETH:

Yikes, that is not a great reputation to have. Why did Jesus choose to come here? How did we become the lucky planet to receive His one and only bestowal as a mortal body?

MARTHA:

There are a few reasons, not all of them known or understood, but one was to end the Lucifer rebellion once and for all—which, again, we will discuss in depth at a later time. The unfortunate history of being involved in the rebellion (through no fault of your own) has created a situation in which Urantia has become among the top three most difficult planets to come for incarnation. The experience of limitation and suffering on your planet is extreme, to say the least.

BETH:

Out of approximately one trillion inhabitable planets, that's saying something to be among the top three *worst*! Are we earthlings considered to be the "bad guys" throughout the superuniverse?

MARTHA:

No, not at all. Feel no guilt in association with your planet's history. In actuality, you should count yourselves among the luckiest of the lucky in this situation, because such a dark, confused and hopeless place was exactly the perfect choice for Jesus Christ Michael of Nebadon to choose for His one incarnation.

This is because it provided the best contrast between your darkness and His message of light. It was the perfect place to reveal the love, forgiveness and mercy of our Creator Father in Heaven.

That being said—take pride in yourself. Only the bravest of the brave come to Urantia. Only those hoping to grow to be the most fully rounded and expanded beings they possibly can, make this journey. A single mortal lifetime spent on your world accelerates the advancement of spiritual growth on an unimaginable scale. You are truly blessed, strong in faith, and courageous to be here.

Let one more thing be known: Jesus made His single required incarnation here, but He has clearly stated that He will one day return. It is not clear whether He will come back again in a human body or as some expression of Spirit. He fulfilled his one required incarnation, but that is not to say He will not return in a similar form or in an entirely new and different way. We do not know when or how this will happen. We do know that your readiness to receive Him will determine the time of His return. He will return when enough hearts have reached a high enough level of love, forgiveness and mercy towards one another. When this happens, it will be a signal to the entire superuniverse that you are ready to receive His second visit.

My own people believe that The Second Coming of Christ will be nothing more than the end of the ego's rule in most of the minds of humanity and thus bring about its full healing. You will then live in a state of true Oneness and peace with all creation, just as my people do now. There will be no physical "savior" but rather, Christ will work through you, and with you directly as Spirit.

And that, my dear friend, is why this information is coming to you. The excitement and love of an entire superuniverse hangs on your spiritual evolution. It is our great joy that, together, through our union and joint will, we can speed along His return by assisting humanity in overcoming the obstacles to love and kindness that have been holding your planet back in the past. It is time to learn how to make the next evolutionary spiritual leap. It is time to lift the barriers to Love's Presence.

BETH:

Very exciting! But as we discuss the possibility of Jesus one day making a second appearance here, whether in the flesh or as Spirit, for some reason it makes me wonder about hell. I've always said I don't believe in it, but just for everyone else's clarity's sake, can you confirm or deny that for me?

MARTHA:

It is worth noting for those who still may believe in some sort of "divine punishment" that there is no location of a "hell" anywhere in the entire Multiverse. There is no room for punishment in the thoughts of a God who abides in us, knows our reasoning and thoughts and loves us without condemnation or condition. Creating such a place you consider to be hell, would go against God's unconditional Love, which is all-inclusive. This means no one is excluded, regardless of what they think they have done. It cannot be any other way, because God is the First Source and Center and cannot create anything other than what He is, which is eternal love and therefore so are you, as one of His creations.

He is the Only Energy. He is the First Cause. He cannot, by His very nature, exclude anyone.

Therefore, you cannot be excluded for your current religious beliefs, your violent actions, your sexual orientation, or the "guilty" thoughts you may think you have. Nothing excludes you from His love. Nothing that happens in the physical world of time and space is punishable for all eternity. This is because the physical world of time and space has been fabricated by you, and it is not part of true reality, which is comprised of only what is eternal. Therefore, all things in the realm of the physical can be undone because none of it is eternal.

BETH:

But if there is no "hell" to send anyone to, to "teach him or her a lesson," is there no accountability then?

MARTHA:

You are each held accountable, but eternal damnation would teach you nothing. In fact, God is so just, and so merciful, He gives you unlimited chances to learn what you need to in the physical realms.

The point of all experience, whether you call it reincarnation, living serial "lives," or simply think of it as one long extended journey in and out of the world of form, is to progress from your physical, time-bound experiences into the eternal experience of living Love and Light. Again, I am here with you now, to help you move beyond this world and up to the next frequency.

That next level of existence is what we call a mansion world.

The mansion worlds are the learning spheres where you go when you leave your physical bodies and ascend to "heaven." I say that with quotes because the mansion worlds are not *the* heaven. True Heaven exists in the innermost spheres of Havona at the Source and Center of the Grand Universe. It is a place within you. The mansion worlds are just the first stage of ascension through the eternal realms, located in the sixth ring surrounding the central focal point from which our Creator extends Himself.

Let me be clear on this however, the mansion worlds are NOT purgatory. In fact, just as with hell, there is no such place as purgatory, although your limited knowledge of the mansion worlds on your planet is probably where the idea came from.

BETH:

So, a mansion world is basically just the first level of Heaven? When we die, we are really just going the first baby step upward and inward? Can't we ascend from there without coming back here again?

MARTHA:

It is on the mansion worlds that you contemplate what you have learned during your lifetimes on Urantia and the other physical worlds of time and space. It is there that you learn how you can improve in your lessons in love and light. Once you have learned all you can at this level you will progress in vibration and be lifted up to the next experiential level. Let me explain the mansion worlds to you in greater detail to help you understand.

BETH:

Yes, please do!

CHAPTER 19

The Eternal Realms

MARTHA:

The mansion worlds are a beautiful, peaceful place of continued learning, where you each spend all of your time when you are "between" earthly lives. Again, you can call these physical excursions "reincarnations," but they are really just experiences within one uninterrupted continuation of your one living eternal existence.

BETH:

Why do these mansion worlds exist? Why don't we just go straight to Heaven?

MARTHA:

When our Creator decides to create a perfect being, it is done by direct and original creation. These are personalities that do not require an ascension plan. Among these are the guardian angels, divine counselors, and archangels to name a few. These are all beings created as perfect for their job functions from the very beginning. They do not have to ascend to a higher frequency to understand who they are and what their purpose is. No learning is necessary as their self-understanding is complete upon creation.

When it comes to beings such as you and me, we were created as ascending material mortals—which means that our perfection is not realized by ourselves in a single step upon our creation, but rather is realized by us over a period of stages through what is called "morontia life."

"Morontia" is a new word for your world that requires some explanation.

The word "morontia" is a term used to describe the vast levels of existence intervening between the material worlds and the spiritual worlds. It is a sort of "in-between" state as you transition from the physical to the non-physical realms. Individuals experiencing a physical existence, such as your people and mine, are thus referred to as "morontia beings" by the upper realms.

BETH:

Now this brings me back to something you said you would explain later. Why would we choose to come to the physical realty of time and space to begin with? Why would anyone ever choose to leave the joyful existence of the eternal realms?

MARTHA:

And this is an excellent place to answer that question in full.

Again, you were created as an "ascending material mortal," meaning that you cannot fully realize your perfection as an eternal creation in a single step. You were created this way out of love, in that such an existence allowed you the choice to experience yourself in whatever way you desired. In this, you were given complete and total free will. We are freewill creatures. No other eternal creation of God is given the choice to do this; neither angels nor any other celestial being.

Angels and other divine eternal creations know who they are from the moment their personality comes into existence. They are not given any other choice to be anything else.

Because morontia beings, such as ourselves, were given the choice to experience creation from any perspective we desired, we chose the most extreme perspective we could imagine: separation from the Mind of our Source.

This idea was incredibly exciting to all creation—though it was but a tiny insane idea, made in an instant, infinitely small in comparison to eternity. This idea was insane in that it is impossible to truly separate oneself from Source. It is the one thing our Creator cannot do; He will never remove your personality from All Totality once you have been created. You will exist forever and anon as an eternal personality who is part of a greater magnificent infinite whole.

In order to experience what you are not—as separate from Source—a disparate "false" reality had to be invented where this could take place, for the eternal realities could not support such an experience.

And so it happened that the outer seventh ring of physical reality, time and space was formed, which you experience as still forming out of this one small thought; a tiny imagining of what it might be like to be something "other" than what you were created to be.

BETH:

So that was the "big bang" then? Trying out our "little thought of separation?"

MARTHA:

Yes, that is an accurate assessment. An unimaginably vast level of experiential creation erupted out of Source in response to your request. This is also why you are each born with "amnesia" regarding where you came from and who you were before you entered into your physical bodies. Should you retain even a small fraction of that eternal memory, you would not attain the full experience of separation and would instantly return to the realms of eternity.

That being said however, it is also the goal of all morontia beings to regain their eternal memory, but organically. It must be your honest desire and heartfelt choice to return to Source while still immersed in the physical realm. You desired to make this level of existence, and now it must also be your choice to let it go—thus unmaking it.

This is not achieved through physical death of the body. Suicide will get you nowhere but more experience of the physical. This is a choice that must be made out of loving service to all creation—the desire of your heart to rejoin with Who You Are in truth, which is a state of oneness with All That Is: It is the state of Atonement.

BETH:

Okay this is really shedding some light on things for me now, but I need one thing you said clarified. Can you please explain to me what you mean by our seventh ring reality being "false?"

MARTHA:

The morontia beings—you and I included, though you do not remember being part of the choice—desired to make a reality without God. However, since true separation from Source is impossible, we morontia beings were given His Great Power to make a world where we only seemed to be sovereign of ourselves. We each forgot our connection to Source and willed into creation a false place where everything in it is in direct opposition to the way things are in the eternal realms. You could say we morontia beings went against God's Will. However, this choice was merely a mistake, not something that can actually be done in truth, and therefore warrants no condemnation. You had God's blessing to try, otherwise He would not have given you the power to do so. You can do nothing, ever, that warrants God's condemnation, for I cannot state enough that separation from our Creator is impossible. You have never actually done what it appears you did. Separation is not real and therefore the reality you are currently experiencing is not real.

And so out of this choice to make a place in opposition to the joy, peace and unity of God's Will, a reality erupted that was everything eternity is not. However, God would never let His children truly harm themselves, and so such a place can never be real—by "real" I mean eternal. Nothing in your world will last forever, even your sun and all the stars will one day expire. It is a reality born to one day die. It is a reality where you can do and be and make as you wish, but none of it will ever last, even as your body must also one day die. And neither are there any consequences to the truth of Who You Are—you are eternal and perfect and whole. This can never be changed but you can play games like children where you pretend to be what you are not in a world with a body that will dissolve with time.

BETH:

So, this seventh ring of reality, which is the experience of physical time and space, is really sort of like one big sandbox?

MARTHA:

Indeed, that is an accurate analogy. We will come back to that idea later. For now, consider this: Have you not wondered why God would throw you into a world of suffering? Why your planet is so filled with hate, revenge and sorrow? That is because none of it was His idea—it was yours and you came here voluntarily. Many of you feel punished by God; while the entire time you suffer, He wills only that you rejoin His Will for peace and love. This reality is not God's will. He did not create it. We morontia beings made it out of the decision to experience separation, which is the opposite to the unity of God's Love. The only way out is to choose only love.

BETH:

I can't believe we would collectively make such a stupid mistake. As wise eternal morontia beings, why would we choose the most extreme experience possible?

MARTHA:

It was indeed a mistake, but a glorious and wonderful one and it can be, and is, already undone. Since time and eternity are two separate realities, in eternity, the separation was merely a half-heartbeat in existence and the mistake was instantly corrected. But in time, this reality is unfolding over untold eons. You can remain in it, maintaining it for as long as you choose, or you can make the decision to ascend.

Do not feel guilty for choosing the experience of the separation! Through the decision to separate all of creation is learning and growing. The ascension of the morontia beings is the most magnificent process ever created. All aspects of eternal creation are involved in assisting those on the path of ascension through the seven rings of reality until Havona Itself is reached. This collective choice to experience what you are not and return to Who You Are was the most efficient and exciting way to achieve total Self-knowing for All Creation.

BETH:

Even so, I'd love to know more about how to turn things around and ascend from this seventh level of reality as quickly as possible.

MARTHA:

You claim your power to undo what you have chosen through being vigilant only for thoughts in alignment with the peace and love of God's Kingdom—the eternal realities. By accepting you have the power to make such a change in your thinking, you will learn to remember what you are. You will remember how to create a reality out of your thoughts. To create, is to love and what you create with love lasts forever in eternity, but not in time. Therefore, you must live in time as though you are already in eternity. Eternity is your true reality because God created you as an eternal being. Nowhere else will ever feel like home to you.

Again, as I stated near the very beginning of these dialogues, forgiveness is the key to returning to the eternal realities. It is the answer to escaping the hell you have made out of your physical reality.

BETH:

I know we talked about it earlier, but can we go over what it means to forgive one more time? I feel I can never be reminded enough.

MARTHA:

To forgive is to overlook. It is to see beyond the false forms you have donned as bodies you think you are now, and instead, know there is a light within that can be seen with your true inner sight. This is your true Eternal Identity. A body will die, but never will this light.

Forgiveness is the acknowledgment of this truth behind all things. For though you cannot see the light with your bodily eyes, the Power of God which you used to make your false reality lies behind all things in it. Therefore, there can be no order of difficulty in forgiving any part of it. In fact, it must all be forgiven equally and totally in order for you to be free of it.

If you want a thought that can bring you quick release and instant peace with the world you currently see, think of these words:

I am blessed as a holy Creation of God in that I have the power of decision to see beyond all barriers I have placed between myself and the awareness of Love's Presence through forgiveness of them. Amen

CHAPTER 20

Life After Death

BETH:

So, what is it like in the next level of reality—is it the sixth ring counting inward from seven to one towards our Source and Center or "ground zero?" And did you say that as we progress forward (inward) all other realities are eternal, existing outside of physical time and space?

MARTHA:

First, let me once again attempt to clarify how the levels of reality are arranged so that you get the clearest picture in your mind of the progression of a morontia soul. However, keep in mind, I am greatly limited in what I can describe. Again, not because it is a secret but, in this case, it is due to your limited grasp of reality and the limitations of the human language as well as the current condition of your mind in general.

The Grand Universe, which contains all seven superuniverses, is made up of many levels of existence in many forms. The only form that is not eternal is the physical one you currently appear as. All other forms you will attain hereafter will simply adapt to your personality, as it changes and evolves in love and light. No other form or identity you will ever assume henceforth will "die" in the way you experience the loss of your physical form in your current reality.

Each of the seven levels of reality can be grouped into a generalized category, as you move inward on your spiritual journey.

The seventh outer ring is the very farthest you can exist in vibration from the awareness our Father Creator. The seventh ring is at the very base level of reality—the ring of physical mortal existence, time and space. So, you could say that the seventh ring is at the very bottom of the rung on the ladder of spiritual progression. You can only go up from there. This ring or level of existence leads up to, but does not include, a planet's settlement in light and life—which is the transition of a physical world into an eternal reality. My planet is currently in the process of making this transition. Soon, ours will be a reality incorporated into the eternal realms or level six.

Level six, as we move inward, is a state where morontia beings exist who are in the process of completing their physical experience careers. At this stage, they have fully committed to their eternal identity and are working towards assuming this identity on a permanent basis. Let it be understood that this transition is not just limited to individuals. Entire universes each one day will attain this first eternal level. This is also where the mansion worlds exist, which indeed is where you will arrive upon physical death of your current body. At this level, you may still choose to go back to the seventh ring, and if so, your spirit may travel back and forth as many times as necessary into a physical body in order to complete your learning.

Levels five progressing on inward to one, as you spiritually evolve towards Havona life at your Center, become more difficult to explain. These are transcendental orders of reality. I find no words in your human language to describe them to you in a meaningful or relatable manner. You have nothing in your current reality with which to compare these lofty existences beyond the outer seventh reality of physical time and space. Such realities are completely opposite to the reality you are living in now. For now, simply accept that joy, love and beauty beyond anything you can imagine await you in these upper levels.

Now, as I stated a moment ago, upon physical death of the body, you will arrive in the sixth ring of reality or the first of the eternal realities which is comprised of the seven mansion worlds. When you make the transition from your Urantia reality to the first mansion world, you will notice a dramatic contrast between the two. The first mansion world truly is paradise compared with what you are experiencing now.

On most planets, the recently departed resume their lives just where they left off when death overcame their physical form. If

Urantia had had a more normal planetary evolution, you would hardly notice you had even "died," except for the fact that you would have a new form.

BETH:

What do you mean by "more normal planetary evolution? Are you referring again to our involvement in the Lucifer Rebellion?

MARTHA:

Yes, Urantia's default into the rebellion caused your planet along with 36 others, to become greatly inhibited in many ways; the most debilitating being your stunted spiritual growth.

BETH:

So, if we came from a planet that had not defaulted into rebellion, when we died, we would simply notice a new type of body and think nothing of it; our lives would simply continue on as before death?

MARTHA:

Yes. On other worlds, death of the body is not perceived with the sense of fear, permanent loss and sorrow as you see on Urantia.

But since Urantia is not a normal planet, you will notice a greater difference between lives lived here versus life on the first mansion world. It is truly heavenly compared with your existence on this world.

Birth and death of the body is not a "beginning" or an "end" to life, but rather just a continuation of your life in a different form. Death is no real change at all. The word "reincarnation" does not exist in the language of most other worlds.

On each mansion world, you will experience progressive spiritual learning as you move inward from level one to seven. And as you progress through your physical experiences on Urantia, you will arrive on any one of these seven worlds—depending on where you left off in your spiritual advancement—each time you transition from a bodily identity.

I will give you a brief description of what to expect on each of these seven mansion world realities within the sixth ring of existence:

MANSION WORLD ONE:

The first mansion world is where you will resume your spiritual learning if you are still at or near the beginning of your lessons in love and light. Nearly all of your training on mansion world one concentrates on where your personality is deficient and in need of correction and healing.

While you are on these mansion worlds, you are by no means alone. You are each assigned guides, known as Morontia Companions. These are not yet your guardian angels—we will discuss these glorious beings in a chapter all their own—but are similar in their helpfulness to you, and equally as loving. You will find companionship with them to be most enjoyable and fulfilling.

Mansion world one also contains the resurrection hall, which is the place many of you who have crossed and returned have described. It is the meeting place where there gather your previously transitioned loved ones to meet you upon arrival after your own physical death.

Mansion world one also holds the Akashic records. These records contain the transcripts and memories of all that transpired during your physical lifetime experiences. It is here that seraphic destiny guardians collectively store and keep such memories safe for you.

From there, when learning is sufficient, you progress on to mansion world two of the training spheres.

MANSION WORLD TWO:

On this sphere or level of existence, you become less physical as your energetic frequency rises, but you will still have some type of tangible body. Though this body is much less dense, your need to eat, drink and rest will remain until all seven levels are completed. However, the type of food you eat and what you drink will be unlike anything you understand now. You will partake of an order of food from God's Kingdom—a type of "living energy." From this living energy, your body will absorb and fully utilize everything it needs. There will be no waste.

On mansion world number two, all types of inner conflict are healed. Anything that has caused you disharmony in the past will be let go of for all eternity.

Here you also begin to intermingle with different orders of celestial beings and form working groups with them to further your spiritual advancement.

MANSION WORLD THREE:

This world is the headquarters of the Mansion World Teachers. Though they help you on all of the seven worlds, sphere three is where they maintain their group headquarters.

There are literally millions of Teachers on each mansion world. They are considered highly advanced cherubim and are with you all through your mansion world career. And when it is time for you to graduate from the mansion worlds, they will be the last to see you off and bid farewell as you sojourn on in your spiritual ascent. The farewell is not permanent. You will meet up with them again near the end of your inward journey.

On the third mansion world, you really begin your progressive learning in truth, light and love. You will begin to learn in depth your relationship to the rest of the cosmos and your universe relationships with other beings.

MANSION WORLD FOUR:

Here new vistas of grandeur open up to you as your mind continues to expand and ascend.

On this sphere you begin to fully understand your place within the superuniverse. You will participate in social activities unknown and unexplainable with words in any language on your planet. All interaction with other beings on this sphere is based on unconditional love, gratitude and willingness to serve others with true joy and freedom. Your motivation to continue to perfect in Divine Love and Goodness will continue to increase as you become progressively more conscious of God—as you experience your direct connection to Him more deeply.

MANSION WORLD FIVE:

Once you reach this level of attainment, you will get a foretaste of what it is like to live on a world settled in light and life; on a planet under normal evolution. The goal of every physical world is to settle in light and life—a state of near heavenly attainment by all inhabitants and their surrounding environment.

On mansion world five you truly become universe minded and acquire an expanded vision of creation at large. It is here that you realize that something truly miraculous and wondrous awaits you at the end of your long, joyful journey inward. Your enthusiasm for ascension will greatly magnify.

MANSION WORLD SIX:

Here ascenders learn more about the other high beings and celestial spirits who exist within the superuniverse, although you may still not be able to see many of them.

You also begin your preparations for graduation from the mansion worlds themselves and the beginning of a new spiritual career. I referred to this as your coronation day earlier in our dis-cussions—your crowning achievement as a morontia being.

It is here you will be taught about the organization of the universe and its guiding beings.

By this time, you will have lost all vestiges of your physical lifetimes and fully accept your place within the One Mind of God, thus fusing with Him in a conscious way that does not ever allow you to forget Him again. You will truly become one with the Holy Spirit within you.

When this happens, you will receive a simple but profound cer-emony of recognition comprised of your supervising superangel for resurrection, archangel, and your dear morontia friends.

At this time, you are still partially material; you are not quite fully spirit yet. But you have come a long way; you are now just below the order of angels at this stage.

MANSION WORLD SEVEN:

Here you reach the pinnacle of your physical experience as a mortal being. On this mansion world, all differences between you and physical beings from other planets are completely lost.

Your journey so far has been as individuals, but now you will begin a new journey and leave in groups as you begin your journey to your next destination: Jerusem—your system capital which exists in the next vibrational level inward towards your Source and Center, the fifth ring of existence: level five.

You will tremendously enjoy your ascent through these seven mansion worlds, as you slowly become less material and more spirit. During your time spent on any one of these mansion worlds, you may choose, for various reasons, to return to a physical identity and planetary experience such as you are doing now. You can do this right up until, and extending through, your seventh mansion world visit. After you complete your journey through the seven mansion worlds, however, typically only those with a specific task assigned to them ever return in the physical to the seventh ring of time and space. Such was tasked Christ Michael, and a few select others who have returned for special teaching missions throughout Urantia's history. You will know them as Buddha, Machiventa Melchizedek, Dalai Lama, Muhammad and many others in your recorded histories.

BETH:

This is all quite amazing and a lot to take in. You are bringing to light many things that will take my mind time to adapt to and accept. Heaven is a much larger place with a lot more going on than I ever imagined.

I have a question though. If you're allowed to tell me, which mansion world will I arrive on when I leave my physical experience here?

MARTHA:

If you physically died right at this moment, you would arrive on mansion world five, where you have very nearly completed your lessons. Soon after your arrival, you would graduate to mansion world six. Keep in mind however, this status can be changed at any time throughout your physical life. There is one thing you each can do while here on your worldly sojourn, that will jettison you directly to mansion world seven upon your physical death. You can practice true forgiveness with all the sincerity of your heart, and upon death, arrive directly within the loving bosom of God, your Source and Center. Forgiveness erases all lessons, past, present and future, from your earthly career. It eradicates from your heart the desire to exist separate from God, thus purifying your mind to the point of instant maximal learning that you can attain from the physical. You have called this moment the holy instant.

BETH:

Oh yes, *A Course in Miracles* refers to the moment of the "holy instant" repeatedly. So interesting to learn about it within the context of the information you're sharing here with me now.

MARTHA:

Indeed, and it is my great hope that together, through the sharing of this unique perspective from a being such as myself, that we bring many directly to this most sacred and holy instant. Humanity's cry to be released from suffering in a quick and instant manner has been heard. And now God, through His most holy Creations in the universe, is answering.

CHAPTER 21

Angels and Other Helpers

BETH:

Okay, I'm dying to talk about the Lucifer Rebellion, but also about the angels. Can we talk about one of those topics next? Unless you have something else in mind?

MARTHA:

Let us address the role of angels in your morontia ascension journey, then we will arrive at the perfect place to discuss the rebellion.

BETH:

Great! Let's have it.

MARTHA:

Guardian angels are assigned in two ways: in groups or as pairs of individuals. They are indeed very real and very present in your daily lives. In fact, throughout human history they have been the only celestial you have continuously acknowledged; you have never forgotten them, which says much about their personal presence, work, and influence as caretakers.

These personal celestial helpers are officially called Seraphim and are what you regard as the traditional "guardian angel." They are always near you and do much for you that you are unaware of. They have been working here on Urantia since the development of mankind's earliest intelligence.

Not all of you have a "personal" guardian angel, however. This is not because such individuals are unworthy, but rather it is a matter of need. Some intelligence levels need less specific guidance, while others require more, due to that particular mind's receptivity. In other words, the more receptive you are to inner spiritual guidance, the more effective your angel can be in helping you and therefore the more likely you will qualify for your own personal guardian angel who never ceases to minister to you.

This may sound unfair, in that most of you may have assumed everyone received the same level of guidance and that you each had a guardian angel assigned to you no matter what. But there is a big difference between guidance and care. You are all equally cared for, but a personal angel will not be assigned to an individual until such a being is responsive to its personal aid. All this requires is a mind who is open to such communication. It does not matter if you are fully conscious of your inner guidance or not; in fact, it is quite likely you will feel there is no communication going on at all. That is just fine. What is important is that you remain open to the idea that communication is possible. Their job is not to be obvious, but rather, to work in such ways that you merely feel inspired and have no awareness of their positive influence at all.

Most "normal minded" people—those of at least minimal intellectual function—will receive their personal guardian seraphim upon reaching a certain level of spirituality. Your soul must be ready to receive such divine assistance in order for it to be effective. This is usually not a conscious thing; it is usually an unconscious state of mind, whereby the individual is ready and willing to accept celestial help and guidance.

As you each spiritually progress, you will have a multitude of angelic helpers assigned to you in groups, which shift and change as your level of spiritual consciousness changes.

If you are wondering whether or not you have a personal guardian angel, just ask yourself this: have you decided to move in the direction of striving to become a more loving human being? Is it your goal to become like our Creator as much as humanly possible with regard to how you treat others? Whether you think you are successful in doing this or not, does not matter. It is the decision itself that makes you a candidate for personal angelic assistance. Such a powerful spiritual choice will always be divinely supported.

All angels are assigned from a group of volunteers. And each angel is assigned to a human or group of humans based upon the human's needs, in accordance with the skill level and experience of the angel.

Yes, angels need to gain experience and wisdom just as you do. Every being is always evolving and improving itself. Even angels.

Angels develop a deep and affectionate loving relationship with you once they are assigned to you as your helper and will remain so for all eternity.

And if you could comprehend their presence while in your earthly form, you would feel the same towards them. The only emotion the angels do not share with you is fear. They find it somewhat difficult to comprehend your sense of fear and anxiety about the past or future. To them, time is non-existent. There is only now, and there is nothing to fear in the present moment of now. However, they truly sympathize with your feelings of dread; they understand your depression and sadness, hoping always to uplift your minds beyond such wasted thoughts, for such thoughts truly do waste your time and energy.

All seraphim are given individual names and numbers. And as they serve in the universe, each angel is identified by name, number and planet of service, as well their number within any other identifying corps they belong to. These personal spiritual attendees typically also serve you in pairs.

When a pair of seraphim decides to accept assignment to a human soul, they serve that person for the remainder of their life on that planet and the whole of their existence thereafter. Upon death, one angel records the life experiences of that individual to be kept in their care.

However, one of the most important tasks of your guardian angels is the facilitation of communication between you and less detectable celestial entities.

As if angels were not already mostly undetectable to your limited senses, there are a host of other celestial beings interested in your well-being and spiritual growth. However, due to their high vibration, it is very difficult for such spirits and entities to make direct contact with you and so your angels facilitate their communication.

You may experience this communication in many ways, such as simply a deepening of faith, a sense of divine purpose, or a feeling of commitment to a higher power. Know that when such feelings of love for the unseen occur, it is most likely the work of your angel bringing it to your mind from a divine source. They are ever watchful of your readiness to accept such communication.

They are true divine coordinators in your lives. Theirs is a difficult and complex task—making comprehensible what is incomprehensible to a mind immersed in the finite world of the physical. You could say they work as your "mind stimulators," in that they work to inspire your mind to consistently make decisions that will lead you ever closer to God. Again, you are usually consciously unaware of such assistance.

However, do not assume that such guidance will always be towards a life of ease and tranquility. In following their inspiration, you will often be met with what appears to be great failures, challenges and disappointments. Look to these times with an uplifted heart; theirs is the task to set you on the quickest path to joy and peace through overcoming the difficulties of human experience. You will be faced with challenges that require you to muster your courage and make clear moral choices. Often, those times you experience your greatest failures, are in truth your greatest accomplishments.

Your angelic helpers unceasingly work together in perfect harmony to bring you exactly those life experiences that will bring you the greatest spiritual insight and wisdom.

However, they do not directly invade your mind or take possession of your free will and personality. They will not violate your personal choices or decisions. Neither angels nor any other order of being has such power. Human beings cannot be possessed by any entity in all God's creation. Your minds are sacrosanct and completely yours and yours alone. Any signs of "demonic possession" can usually be attributed to a malfunctioning mind or someone who has become so convinced of such false possession that they unconsciously behave in ways they believe are synonymous with it.

Another detail of interest is that angels do not possess wings, as your artists have often depicted. What many have seen but failed to understand, upon the vision of their guardians through the eyes of the flesh, has been but the Great Rays of our Creator, emanating from them in a glorious display. From the perspective of the mortal mind, the only possible translation would be to equate such radiating light with wings.

One thing the angels are not assigned to you to do however, is answer your prayers. Do not try to pray to them, for answering prayers apart from their spiritual mission in helping you grow, is not their function. That is the function of our Creator and Him alone.

One thing you can do, however, is your best to make their job a little easier by being receptive to their care and leading.

They can indeed become physical, though, and help you here on the material plane when such assistance is deemed necessary to your spiritual progress. But these occasions are very rare and unusual, and the circumstances must be considered crucial—certain vital human links in your spiritual evolution are seen as too important to be prematurely severed. You are each here for a reason, and you each play an important part in the larger plan of humanity's awakening, and if some individuals die before completing their appointed task, the chain in your spiritual development may be compromised. And so, to prevent such catastrophes, the angels will, on rare occasion, intervene on your behalf, on the physical plane.

Your guardians will accompany you as open companions once you leave the world of the physical and enter the eternal morontia spheres. They will travel with you from that point on as your constant companions and assistants throughout the rest of your spiritual progression, until you finally reach Havona itself.

And even here, some of these guardians will opt to stay with you, and those who do not, continue on their own path of angelic spiritual attainment. They then later rejoin you on Havona, having completed their own learning as well.

Regardless of what happens, your angels will forever remain in communication with you. Your relationship with them is long and intimate, never to be forgotten or completely severed. You are forever bound to those angels who volunteered to serve as your guardians and counselors, and your love is deep and mutual.

In return for their service to the morontia beings traversing the long spiritual ascent, they gain the inner circles of increasing awareness of our Creator alongside you. For as they successfully guide you on your way, they also gain in wisdom and knowledge of our Source and Center. The assignment of guardian over you is highly sought after.

It is of utmost importance, then, to learn to work with your seraphic guardians; to make their work easier. To do this, you must become good listeners, quiet of mind and peaceful of thought. Then you will feel their presence and be able to follow their inner guidance, and progress as quickly as possible through your trials and lessons in this physical life.

There are many other types of angelic beings besides the order of seraphic guardian. These other orders do not involve themselves directly with your day-to-day activities, as your seraphic helpers do. Theirs is a more indirect role in your ascension plan. The list of them is exhaustive and we will not take the time to discuss them here.

In closing on the topic of angels, let this rest in the forefront of your mind: as you go about your spiritual work here on Urantia, you are being watched over, cared for and assisted by beings so numerous, their numbers are beyond comprehension. Your evolutionary spiritual journey inward towards Havona, through the levels of existence, is a long and exciting one. You will have many other guides and friends to help you along the way, while you, in turn, help those coming up behind you. No creature is greater than another and no being is more important than another; each being is simply at a different stage of learning along their path in life.

That being said, angels are superior to you in spiritual status now, but they neither judge nor accuse you of anything. They minister to you, as God's messengers, and are loving personalities. Keep in mind, that while they are not to be worshiped or prayed to, it is good to love them. They can help you in unimaginable ways as they possess many powers beyond human comprehension. However, it is interesting to know that though they themselves possess such power and majesty, they greatly enjoy your efforts in music, art, and humor. And they are not so far removed from your world in that they also have complete understanding of your struggles and difficulties. They truly love you and make every effort to help you.

There are angels or seraphic hosts for just about every necessary function needed in the Grand Universe, and their numbers are beyond human count. Again, I will not name all the distinct varieties and their functions here, as this would go beyond the scope of what I wish to teach you at this time. Merely understand that like any good leader, God has many helpers working through His guidance who carry out the day-to-day functions of all creation. Rest assured, angels are indeed truly extensions of His Will.

CHAPTER 22

The Lucifer Rebellion

MARTHA:

And now we come to material you have been patiently waiting for me to address: The Lucifer Rebellion.

BETH:

Yes! I'm interested to hear about this from you. I'm sitting on the edge of my seat!

MARTHA:

Well then let us not delay any further.

Many of you have heard mention of the "war in heaven" but you know very little about it. Many of your ancient historical accounts vary, but I assure you, none of them has it entirely correct.

And let it be noted that there is no specific "devil" in existence, as counterpart in power and might to God.

You seem to have lumped all the notorious names known throughout history under the umbrella of one deity, and you simply have termed him "the devil" when no such being has or ever will exist—just as no hell has or ever will exist.

However, it does not mean that such names do not belong to actual personalities involved with what the superuniverse refers to as, "The Lucifer Rebellion." On this point you have been greatly misled and misinformed.

Lucifer was your planet's initial assigned leader, your System Sovereign of 607 inhabited worlds, including Urantia. Though he initiated what later became called "The Lucifer Rebellion," he did not start out with such misguided intentions for your planet or any of the other planets under his care and leadership.

Lucifer had great experience as a leader and possessed an impeccable history of wisdom and beauty. He was considered one of the most brilliant of his order of being, both in intelligence and appearance. His light shone both bright and true; his brilliant personality was near matchless in integrity and grace.

That being said, however, all decision-making personalities of any order have free will, and even the most promising can fall into erroneous thinking.

Lucifer was not the first System Sovereign to "fall" in his thought processes. He was the last of three to have defaulted from God's Will throughout the long superuniverse ages—meaning he rejected his allegiance and relationship with our Father Creator. I say he was the last, because with the visitation of Jesus Christ Michael to your planet, all such nonsense has been completely and everlastingly laid to rest. No other uprising shall ever occur again in the ages to come. All that can be learned from such backward thinking has been taught.

BETH:

So, where did Lucifer go wrong?

MARTHA:

Though he was among the most brilliant beings, this was also his great downfall. His "wrong turn" was down the path of self-aggrandizement. His thoughts "fell" in vibration ever so little in the beginning, but these insidious thoughts took root and grew, eventually corrupting his mind so much so that the light of truth became blocked entirely. He defaulted into selfish-ness instead of self-fullness. With such debased thinking comes behavior to match.

BETH:

Is that what *A Course in Miracles* and other related spiritual teachings refer to as the development of our "ego?" Is that what happened to Lucifer; he developed an ego?

MARTHA:

In a sense, yes. Except he underwent no process of "forgetting" such as each of you experience upon your mortal entry into this world. He had full access to all he needed to stay on the path of love and light. In him, there was no excuse, no reason to fall in his beliefs.

Let it be known that no being, no matter how high their personality in the celestial world, is exempt from the temptation to become self-absorbed and self-exalted. You know from your own personal experience how easy it is to fall into thinking you are better than someone else.

This was the only fault of Lucifer, and such thinking led to his complete and total downfall. Unfortunately, he did not fall alone. Many others soon followed suit behind his long and disdainful descent into darkness.

Satan was among those personalities, as Lucifer's first assistant. He is named after your Local System, Satania.

Your planet knows so very little about these once glorious beings, and it pains me to reveal their names here, knowing how vilified they have become in your minds as "the devil," whom you have painted with evil. Let this teaching be the first to undo what history has taught you in error, as you keep the most open of minds.

However, if you were ever to assign the term "devil" to any being it is Caligastia—your former Planetary Prince of Urantia. He was in commanding jurisdiction just below Satan and instigated and performed much of the "dirty work" of the rebellion here on your planet. Until the last century, his name has been effectively eradicated from your historical accounts due to his abhorrent part in the events that unfolded.

Abaddon was the chief of staff of Caligastia, who too followed his leader into rebellion, and Beelzebub, a leader of the corps of your planetary caretaker beings known as "Midwayers" or "Watchers," many of whom also decided to default into rebellion.

So, you see, there are many names that have been used and confused as one in your planetary history. Such names actually belong to separate individuals who each played a unique part in leading your planet down into isolation and darkness.

However, on a side note, as for the "devil" being associated with the color red, there is a logical explanation. Once Lucifer's vibration began to degrade, so too did his glorious vestiges of brilliant white and golden light, as well as many other beautiful colors, unseen and unknown by the human eye. By the end of his regime, his coloration and that of many of his cohorts, became largely red. Red is the lowest energy of visible light to the human eye. Lucifer gradually degraded to this color as he reflected this, the lowest possible vibration he could become.

BETH:

What caused this rebellion to begin with if these were such perfect and highly exalted beings? Why would anyone turn away from the power, majesty, and perfect peace of God's eternal love? It seems impossible.

MARTHA:

There was no particular cause, no special "trigger" or unique condition that set Lucifer on this path of self-absorbent thinking that led his heart to set a barrier between himself and God. Again, we are all unique creatures and given the free will to decide for ourselves what we want to believe. Lucifer just began a thought pattern that he never saw fit to get out of. No one ever suggested the rebellion to him; he came up with it all on his own.

His was a subtle, gradual fall from grace. His thoughts began to "lower" in that they became a lower quality than ones previous and thus of a lower frequency. This is why his descent is called a "fall" from grace. His thoughts literally lowered to only those thoughts surrounding himself. In this way, anyone can become "self-centered" or "selfish." When your thoughts are in a state of grace, your thoughts extend to the wellbeing of others besides yourself, and are thus of a higher, expanded quality and there-fore a higher vibration. Higher thoughts are all thoughts that are above "self." They are thoughts of Oneness, not separation and isolation. In its simplest form, it is the idea that you feel com-pelled to treat others with loving kindness because that is how you would like to be treated by them in return.

As Christ Michael once admonished your world: "Do unto oth-ers as you would have them do unto you." This truly is the Golden Rule by which all thinking should be governed.

Lucifer's thinking simply began with a mild dissatisfaction with the whole universe ascension process. He never openly criticized the universe process of spiritual evolution, but he stewed about it for what would equal about one hundred years of time. Throughout this time, Lucifer sank deeper and deeper into his personal complaints about the entire mortal ascension plan. The official beginnings of open rebellion are unclear, but it is known that the rebellion began in this way within Lucifer's own mind. He had an overall feeling of being controlled or "locked in" by the governing rules of the eternal realities. He felt he had no personal freedoms aside from assisting with the ascension plan of morontia beings.

Once the rebellion was openly started, the rebels named it the "Lucifer Declaration of Liberty."

The idea the rebels never embraced or understood is that they had been free all along. Their liberty was never at stake. There was never any need to rebel against anything because the whole of creation is, and always will be, totally free. The fact that they were allowed to rebel without restraint to begin with is clear evidence of this supreme truth.

Whatever their blindness to the truth, the rebels outlined three parts to their cause and complaint about the way the universe was being run:

1. They decided that the Universal Father of All Creation was a fictitious personality. Such a being did not exist and that creation would have come about regardless of His existence. Creation was inherent in itself. They also denied that such a Creator had any part in their own creation and was not a part of themselves. Their personality and creation were not a gift from God. However, Lucifer does not go on to explain, then, where such forces for creation originated from if it were not from our Source and First Cause, God the Father. It appeared to the rest of the superuniverse that his self-absorption and low vibrational thinking did not allow his mind to move beyond his own self-inflicted restrictions. He could not think beyond his own theories and ideologies.

2. Lucifer also contested the rule of Christ Michael over superuniverse 7, mandated by a fictitious, hypothetical Creator Father. He made this claim based solely on the fact that none of the lower orders of being, himself included, could

actually perceive our Creator. He went on to accuse Christ Michael of self-aggrandizement for assuming such a role.

As is even true on your planet today, the blind eye only sees what is reflected within its own mind.

Lucifer insisted that immortality and the continuance of spirit were inherent traits of all beings. Life went on in an "automatic" fashion.

Again, he never went on to qualify exactly where or how such "automatic" creation came from. His theory did not allow for any postulations beyond his own reasoning. He simply insisted, out of sheer stubbornness, that we had no connection to a Source or Higher Power.

3. Lucifer felt that the amount of energy and effort poured into the plan for mortal ascension was an overall waste. He contended that our overall destiny was unknown and perhaps a purely fictitious promise. He proposed that our future was merely a dead end.

He made this claim simply because he did not know God's overall plan for morontia beings and had apparently lost patience in waiting to find out.

Lucifer was given free rein to test his ideas and continue the rebellion for about 200,000 years of Urantia time.

I would like to point out here that your planet is among those representing the direct result of Lucifer being given full freedom to test his claims and wishes.

Your world is a dark disaster because of decisions made by Lucifer and his rebels. As stated earlier in this discourse, out of about one trillion inhabitable planets in our superuniverse, yours is deemed among the top three worst planets to incarnate on.

On a normal planet of typical evolution, the people are usually integrated with the rest of the inhabitable planets of the superuniverse by now. By this time of your planetary evolution, the people of Urantia should not only be fully aware of other evolved physical beings from other planets in your physical reality, but also your guardian angels as well as a myriad of other helpful beings that constantly watch and help you and all living things.

Yet because of the God-given total freedom and independence bestowed upon each personality, Lucifer was allowed to do as he pleased for about 200,000 years. This gave him enough time to demonstrate his views and allow for full fruition of his plan for both mortals and angels alike.

Such behavior did not go unnoticed, however. The archangel Gabriel was keeping a close eye on things, though he did not interfere with the Will of God. Loyalty to God's Will is voluntary and chosen; it cannot be forced upon anyone. Freedom is demonstrated by the ability to choose and Gabriel chose to be still and watch only.

The very fact Lucifer was allowed to go on his way for as long as he did, should have been glaring proof of the truth of the freedom he so vehemently claimed he did not have.

But there was a limit.

The rebellion had been confined to just the system of Satania. And even though it was contained to just 37 inhabited planets, it was a time of tribulation, testing and confusion of all beings involved.

Michael our Creator Son, after counsel with his Paradise brother Immanuel, decided to deal with the conflict as He had the other two in the past; an attitude of noninterference and full allowance of free will towards Lucifer's rebellious actions.

And so, the "war in heaven" began, as it became divided between those who still willed to be joined as One in God's Name and those who chose to separate and strike out on their own. Just as with any official conflict, each side had a banner associated with it.

Christ Michael's was three azure blue concentric circles on a white background, representing the Holy Trinity or Trinity government of all creation.

Lucifer's banner emblem was a white background with one red circle, and a black solid circle in the center.

This was not a war as you may conceive of it on Urantia. This was an individual internal battle of moral decision for each personality. Those who doubted their beliefs would often waver back and forth from light to dark, uncertain of which path to follow until a final choice was made. There was no physical fighting or sword battle, but rather a long and drawn out verbal display between Lucifer and Gabriel as each pleaded their case for righteousness and truth.

Because there was no destruction do not be misled in thinking that this was a trivial debate. It was very easy for some of the naiver beings to be bedazzled by Lucifer's visual radiance versus their own internal faith, dependent upon the experience of a God Who was still unseen to them.

It took many great courage and strength not to be led astray.

Thankfully there were only 37 planets involved in the rebellion, or the "Declaration of Liberty," as proclaimed by Lucifer. And with such a declaration of separation came the consequences of willfully seceding from God.

All planets whose Princes defaulted and joined the rebellion were thusly cut off—quarantined—from all outside communications with the rest of the superuniverse planets.

Under normal conditions, your planet would receive system "broadcasts" and other types of interplanetary communications from the "outside" worlds. The suspension of communication was done to prevent Lucifer from spreading the news of the rebellion to any more planets. And these circuits of communication will not be restored while Lucifer—though now detained and restricted, having been stripped of all power—still exists within your System.

Yet, at any time throughout this whole rebellion, all Lucifer would have had to have done was accept God's grace, love and forgiveness and he would have been saved.

In fact, mercy had been offered him and his rebels repeatedly by Christ Michael, and every time this offer was extended, Lucifer and many of his followers refused it all the more vehemently.

Know this: God will always accept you back into His fold no matter what. His patience and love are without end. He will never abandon you, but if you abandon Him, there is nothing He will do to stop you. This is your free will and free choice.

Take comfort in this though—just because you are here on this planet, does not mean you personally fell into rebellion. The

fact that you are here now, is clear evidence you successfully survived the rebellion. This is because all rebels have been detained
and placed under quarantine since the bestowal visit of Christ Michael on Urantia some 2000 years ago. They are now being held
on one of the seven "detention worlds" awaiting final adjudication
and have no power to corrupt the love of God within anyone's
heart ever again.

CHAPTER 23

The End of the Rebellion

BETH:

So, what happens next for Lucifer and the other rebels? I can't imagine they will be detained for all eternity.

MARTHA:

No, they will not. Currently, the superuniverse awaits the final decision in what you could call the "Gabriel versus Lucifer" trial. It is believed that all rebels who will ever accept God's mercy have now done so. It is anticipated that all rebels who currently still refuse His mercies will eventually choose to be "unmade." This is a state in which the defaulted personality created by God is reabsorbed into the Whole in such a way as they never again remember their former selves as they once were. It is supposed that once this happens, such beings will then be recreated again anew, into a new version of their former selves. They will have an entirely fresh beginning with no memory of their former existence. Neither will anyone recognize them as they once were. Again, this is a personal choice, not a verdict or punishment mandated by God or any other celestial being. It is the free will choice made by one who cannot go on as they are, having reached a state of complete stalemate with the truth of their being. It is the decision to be completely unwilling to accept the love and light of their own existence. Such a being will not be "unmade" until all trace of light and love are completely absent in them. God will allow as much time as necessary for this decision to come to pass in the mind of one so fallen; and mercy will be instantly extended in the event they change their mind, right up until their final decision is carried out.

Though the idea of being "unmade" may sound somewhat disconcerting to you, understand that it is a very rare occurrence. In a superuniverse comprised of untold numbers of beings, beyond the human ability to count, this seldom takes place. It is virtually unheard of. It is the most merciful outcome for a being who is unwilling to move forward and heal from their mistakes.

But do not ever fear to make mistakes! It is through our greatest mistakes that our greatest lessons may yet be learned.

The Lucifer rebellion was indeed a great mistake, having caused the greatest upheaval in the history of our superuniverse and affecting more beings than any other negative event. Yet, now it has been determined by the higher celestial beings that the good that has come of it is more than a thousand times greater than the sum of its initial negative consequences.

However, because your planet has been misled by a corrupt Planetary Prince for so long, you as a people are quite spiritually confused; you cannot distinguish between what is true and what is false, spiritually speaking.

Christ Michael has begun to set this information straight through His physical visitation to your planet and in many other ways since then, through many other channels.

Yours is a world based upon falsity; a place where what is true is obscured by what is false. Perhaps you could say Urantia and the other 36 defaulted planets are "twice fallen." The first "fall" came with the decision of all morontia beings to make an illusory existence for themselves in the form of the seventh outer ring of physical time and space to experience separation from Source, and the second "fall" manifested in the form of the rebellion—an even greater step away from Union with Source.

However, remember this: it is impossible to sever oneself entirely from the Source of your Life Energy. You can forget so deeply that it will seem as though it were true, and with such forgetting, comes the experience of lack of total communication with not only your Divine Creator, but with the entire superuniverse itself.

On a normal planet existing in the illusory world of physicality, your experience would have been vastly different from your Urantia life. On most planets, physical beings have an overall delightful, peaceful and happy learning adventure when they arrive along the timeline at your stage of development. Most beings look forward to their journey with a physical body and the diverse learning that can be attained through it. They are completely aware their physical reality is not a real one; it is lived much like a child would play in a sandbox—an analogy we have mentioned before and will come back to in full at the end of these dialogues, through a special presentation. Such beings fear nothing of their physical experiences and enjoy the camaraderie of their fellows there with them; again, much like happy children playing make-believe in a sandbox. While their emotions and reactions to life are very real lessons for them, they know at the end of the day, theirs is not a real world. Lessons in love are learned more easily when taught through joy instead of suffering.

Lucifer was truly blinded by his own self-glorification and you would have continued to suffer under his selfish leadership indefinitely if Christ Michael had not mercifully brought the rebellion to an end. No planet shall ever be deprived of its own evolution through another's poor decisions.

But know this, no matter how much you have suffered as a result of the wrong choices and misdeeds of those who should have been lovingly guiding you—it was all only temporary. You are now free of such tyranny, but you have a long way to go to overcome the damage that has been done. There is still much darkness on your planet, and not all of it stems from yourselves alone. Visiting dark-energy races who have mettled with humanity for thousands of years from other planets are currently being eradicated. But do not fear, you have also been visited by light-energy races from other planets, who have assisted and kept careful watch over Urantia for eons. And soon they will step forward fully into your reality as part of your ascension plan. It's time to meet your neighbors and friends from other parts of the galaxy who love you so much.

And know this; there is a beautiful compensation for the suffering you have endured here on Urantia.

Because of the particularly difficult trials of living on Urantia, this world puts out some of the most loving, compassionate, merciful and forgiving souls the superuniverse has ever seen. Yours is an unprecedented journey. Your spiritual careers from here on will be magnified and glorified in such a way that could not be achieved on any other planet. You who live here and learn to triumph over hate and fear with love and light will go on to do great things in the Name of God.

All beings have a purpose and should not be viewed as "good" or "bad" but rather, merely as part of the necessary experiences brought to you for your own benefit. Let your heart not hold a grudge against Lucifer. God and all those loving celestial beings that serve Him are not seeking revenge for any unfair treatment; they do not desire to punish Lucifer and his rebels, but only to extend them the mercy and love they would extend themselves. Even in the face of what could be deemed a great misdeed, and a ruinous mistake, the "Golden Rule" still prevails. As I stated previously, it truly is the rule that governs all living. It is the universal ideal of all relationships in the grand universe:

Treat others as you believe God would treat them and as you would have yourself be treated.

CHAPTER 24

The Visitation of Adam and Eve

MARTHA:

And now it is time to set right the events of a particularly misunderstood era in your planet's history: The visitation of Adam and Eve.

BETH:

Yes! Let's talk about this! The "creation story" is so strange and mystical to me. Tell me what really happened.

MARTHA:

Contrary to what your bible and many other traditional "creation story" accounts depict, your world was not created in seven days and Adam and Eve were not the first humans to inhabit the planet.

What these stories have become throughout the ages as they were passed down from generation to generation through oral recitation, is nothing more than a conglomerate of facts combined with fiction to "fill in the blanks," so to speak. No one is to be faulted; it was merely how things proceeded. Now we are going to set right these misunderstood events of long ago.

As stated earlier, humans evolved from a single living cell, brought into life through the Life Carriers who seeded your planet with the energy of the Living Father. Your journey, and the journey of all life currently inhabiting your planet, has been long indeed from that exciting moment ages ago!

No being native to your planet has ever suddenly appeared, fully created by God. Such events are natural to the realms of eternity, but never in time. And so, all native things come into existence on your planet in their own time. Such is the nature of life in the seventh ring of existence in the realm of physical time and space.

Every planet's inhabitants, at some point, reach their full capacity for genetic development. Meaning, physically a species has come as far as it can go from the standpoint of physical evolution on their own. Spiritually speaking, a planet's inhabitants could be anywhere along the road in development, but their bodies have reached an endpoint.

About 40,000 years ago, you, as a human race, reached that point.

After inspection of your physical "readiness" by the Life Carriers, it was determined that the human race was now ready to receive a Material Son and Daughter.

The purpose of receiving a Material Son and Daughter is to bring a genetic uplift to the human race, so that you may continue to evolve and improve as a species as well as receive a greatly enhanced understanding of the spiritual truth of Who You Are.

You find evidence of their visit in your biblical story of Adam and Eve. But there is little remaining truth to be found in it. The bible errs in citing their arrival as the beginning of the human race; their visitation was merely the next stage in your evolution that began millions of years earlier.

The Material Sons are always called "Adam" and the Material Daughters are always called "Eve." The names "Adam" and "Eve" actually denote an order of celestial being, not individual people. Just as you are referred to collectively as the ascending Sons of God, these beings are collectively referred to as "Adams" and "Eves."

And so as just stated, every inhabited planet at some point in their physical evolution, receives a visit from a Material Son and Daughter—an Adam and an Eve—for a genetic and spiritual uplift, to continue development as a species.

I would like to add a side note here, that there has been much manipulation of the human genome done uniquely on Urantia throughout history by other races from other planets in the physical realm. Some have done this with good intensions and others deeply nefarious. This was allowed as part of the freedom given throughout the Lucifer Rebellion but is now being ended.

Resuming my narrative, again, only a small portion of the original Adam and Eve story persists after nearly 40,000 years of being passed along from generation to generation. However, given your planet's descent into darkness, it is really quite remarkable that any of it survived at all.

This much is true however: there was a mistake made, and there was a real place called "The Garden of Eden," but beyond that, we reach the end of the main similarities between the truth and fiction.

And now, I bring you the rest of that story.

On a normal planet, the coming of a Material Son and Daughter brings great advancement in culture and civilization. There are advancements in invention, intellect, and great spiritual enlightenment. On these worlds this is usually what is considered to be a "Golden Age."

This was not achieved on Urantia. To date, only rare pockets of civilizations have achieved their own personal "Golden Age" throughout history but, to date, there has not yet been any such worldwide "Golden Age" during any time of your planet's history. But I promise, one is coming and is nearly at hand.

Though you were physically ready to receive a genetic and social uplift, you were far behind spiritually speaking. In fact, the rebellion set you so far back, that you were still in the dark ages of spiritual understanding.

Under Lucifer's leadership, there had been no lasting forward progress on your world with regard to your spiritual enlightenment. With few exceptions, most humans were still very savage towards one another at the time of the arrival of your Adam and Eve.

After it had been announced to your planet that you would receive an Adam and an Eve, nearly 100 years passed before they actually arrived. This time lag was given so that a place could be prepared in advance for their arrival. On normal planets, the announcement that an Adam and Eve are being sent motivates the population of an entire world to prepare a place for their reception and permanent residence.

In Urantia's case, most of the world lived in spiritual darkness, so there were few who understood what this announcement meant, and even fewer who were willing to help. Just over 3,000 workers were recruited to assist in the building of the beautiful garden dwelling that was to be the home of your beloved Adam and Eve.

The location for this garden was on a long narrow peninsula off the Mediterranean that extended far out to the sea, near what you call Mesopotamia today. The climate there, at that time, was ideal and consistently mild and warm.

On your planet, at that time, there truly existed what was referred to as "The Tree of Life." It was a type of plant, the only one of its kind, that stored energies which were age-defying for those who had physical bodies prepared for them from the eternal realms, to be used in the seventh ring reality. Such bodies were not born on Urantia through physical means, but rather, created "off world." These bodies allowed eternal beings to walk the worlds of physicality, time and space, as any mortal, for as long as they needed to and for as long as they partook of the occasional consumption of its leaves as sustenance. In essence, the tree allowed them to maintain their eternal qualities while living in the physical. The leaves of the plant were able to store and release energy, much like that of a battery, when eaten and processed by certain divine beings indwelling these specifically crafted mortal bodies. Such bodies were not born natives to your world, but rather made-to-order for an eternal being's energy to inhabit, without going through the forgetfulness of the birthing process. That being said, if a native mortal on Urantia were to eat of its leaves, it would be entirely useless to them. In order for the tree to be useful, a being had to be of the right molecular vibration or it would pass right through the body as normal food.

BETH:

So, what eventually happened to this tree? Where is it today?

MARTHA:

After the failure of Adam and Eve's mission on Urantia—which I will recount shortly—everyone left the garden, including Adam and Eve. They were not allowed to take the tree with them when they moved to their new location. Instead, as part of the condition of the failure of their mission, Adam and Eve where henceforth destined to live as normal mortal beings and died a normal mortal death.

The tree itself was eventually destroyed by those who drove Adam and Eve, along with all their followers, from Eden. These savage people ate the leaves of the tree for years and became angry once it was discovered they could gain no extension of life from it. One day, during a local conflict, they burned the tree to the ground.

All that remains of the once glorious Garden of Eden is now but a partial stone wall, long since submerged under the Mediterranean Sea. Eventually the entire land mass was claimed by the sea. The sinking was not sudden as many of your Atlantean tales portray, but rather it took several hundred years to slowly submerge. Neither was this period in history the time when Atlantis existed. Land masses have risen and submerged similarly over the eons, with many comingling tales.

I now feel your questions about Atlantis, but it is a story that diverges from this one, and there are others commissioned to tell it.

BETH:

Okay, I won't ask about Atlantis now then. So, what happened? How did Adam and Eve fail in their mission here?

MARTHA:

Adam and Eve were instructed to remain in the Garden until they had procreated enough children to sufficiently spread around the world, in equal fashion, to all the various peoples and tribes. Their genetic material was to be shared evenly among all the global inhabitants out of fairness. No one people were to become special, and no one group would be allowed a genetic advantage, and thus dominion, over another. Once a sufficient number of "pure-blooded" children had been created, they were to send them out into the world to intermarry with Urantia natives and thus begin the process of integration of upgraded genetic material and the worldwide spread of deepened spiritual teachings.

As you can imagine, carrying out such an endeavor would require much time, patience and foresight.

However, they only partially succeeded before Caligastia interfered and triggered the downfall of these plans.

CHAPTER 25

The Early Days of Adam and Eve

BETH:

How did Adam and Eve arrive here? Were they brought by a spaceship?

MARTHA:

Not quite. Celestial beings do not utilize non-eternal means to travel between the realms. They arrived via "celestial transport," meaning they were brought to Urantia by a transport seraphim. Such beings exist to function as transporting agents for other eternal beings who lack the ability to transfer their life force from reality to reality or from one vibrational existence to a dramatically different one.

Urantia's particular Adam and Eve were specially selected from many thousands of qualified pairs. They accepted the mission to incarnate upon one of the most challenging planets in the history of our superuniverse.

On that first momentous day, they arrived unannounced, and after 10 days, their material bodies were made ready for them to inhabit. These bodies were just over eight feet tall, with blonde hair and beautiful blue eyes—the color of the sky on a clear day. As non-physical beings, such bodies had to be prefabricated for them, since they were not to be "born" onto the planet through the normal means. Rather, they were brought to Urantia in their natural non-physical forms and once there, entered the bodies prepared for them as fully formed and functional.

After transition into their new physical bodies, they regained consciousness simultaneously.

The physical forms of Adam and Eve gave off a light of their own, and it extended out beyond them—much like the light my people are beginning to exhibit now, as we spiritually evolve. In your ancient Sumerian translations, you will find reference to their light. Such texts refer to these visitors as "The Shining Ones."

The light comes from our inner being—our True Self—shining through the thin veil of form. You will find it interesting to know, that while clothing covered most of the light that radiated out from them, there was always a visible "halo" encircling their heads. This is why so many of your artists depict saints and other holy individuals with such a light around their heads in paintings and other work. This is also the reason you portray angels in the same way. Such a halo has truly been seen by mortal eyes when beholding the divine.

Adam and Eve could also communicate telepathically with each other and with their immediate children.

The beings created as Material Sons and Daughters always work in pairs under all circumstances, never to be separated. Very seldom do they work alone. This is important to know because it sheds some light on their actions of self-sacrifice and love as we continue with their tragic story.

Van and Amadon were the first two beings present to welcome Adam and Eve upon their awakening on Urantia. At this time, Van, who had been the spiritual authority and guide of your planet for over 150,000 years, then handed over this responsibility, as well as the care of the Tree of Life to Adam and Eve. He and Amadon were fellow non-native beings of divine origin, much like Adam and Eve, and had sustained their existence indefinitely, until the arrival of Adam and Eve, through consuming food from the Tree of Life. Theirs is a long a beautiful story, but again, off topic here. Simply know that they "carried the torch" so to speak for the continuance of humanity's spiritual development throughout the long dark ages under Lucifer and Caligastia's rule.

The first thing Adam and Eve noticed once they were formally awake and aware of their surroundings was the complete and utter silence of Urantia.

They had been told the planet was being held under quarantine and isolation, cut off from the rest of the superuniverse communications, but nothing could prepare them for the stark reality of truly experiencing the deep silence of it. Having always been in perpetual contact with our Creator and the collective superuniverse communications, the total inner silence, as a result of the rebellion, was a deafening shock. Though they had been thoroughly trained and educated regarding the dire conditions on Urantia, nothing could prepare them for such a feeling of deep separation from God and all creation.

The second day was not much better than the first for uplifting Adam and Eve's spirits, regarding the situation on Urantia. Their associates debriefed them on the full details of the Caligastia rebellion, and it truly began to sink in just how difficult their task was going to be.

The situation was entirely disheartening.

They also realized how tragically off track a planet could become if the normal plan of progression was not followed.

Caligastia had tried to advance the planet technologically without following the spiritual plan of divine progression alongside it. This set up nothing but chaos and repeated catastrophes throughout your planet's history, as spiritually underdeveloped peoples tried to live alongside one another, some with technology far beyond what they could behave responsibly with. Too many races of extraterrestrial beings with dark motives had also been allowed to mettle in your past.

Because of this, often in the past, the world suffered near cataclysmic scenarios, nearly wiping out humans altogether. And each time, humans had to start all over again nearly at the beginning.

On the third day Adam and Eve took a tour of the entire Garden. They did this from the backs of the great passenger birds called fandors that lived on your planet during this time. They had a wingspan of 24 feet, and the pair rode them high above the Garden, surveying all that lay below. It truly was the most beautiful place on Earth at that time. The inspection ended with a banquet in honor of all those individuals who worked so hard to build the magnificent Garden.

On the fourth day, Adam and Eve held an assembly to officially inform the inhabitants of their forthcoming plans for Urantia's spiritual and physical evolution. This forum ended with another great feast in celebration of the coming glad times.

On the fifth day, they began to organize and delegate specific tasks which laid the foundation for the new planetary government.

On the sixth day, Adam and Eve were escorted around the Garden on foot, to more closely inspect the various animals and plants tended there. They noted the great variety of creatures and vegetation that existed on Urantia, some both strange and wonderful, while others quite deadly. Such life struggle between living things only further represented the disorder and chaos of a planet under no moral guidance.

As they walked, Adam, who had studied much of the flora and fauna of Urantia prior to his arrival, named all that he saw. He could also cite their behaviors and function within the greater whole of nature. Eve was almost as proficient, and the people were amazed by this.

On the seventh day, Adam and Eve were nigh exhausted from their efforts to assimilate and assess their situation on Urantia. They had intended to take a day of rest; however, that luxury was not come to pass.

The native people could scarcely process such great and wise beings as Adam and Eve, and throughout the first six days of their time, had been planning to erect a temple of worship for them. They were, indeed, seen as gods among men.

The peace of the tired couple was disturbed, with the news of such activity early in the morning on this seventh day. They immediately went to the temple to address the people.

Once there, Adam admonished them, clarifying that the only being worthy of worship was God the Father, Creator of all things. Though His was an invisible Presence, it was His very Presence that sustained all life, in all its wonderous forms, including Adam and Eve themselves. They were no greater than the lowliest human and were not on the planet to be worshiped, but rather to be learned from.

The people understood and from that day on, the common

tradition you have today of worship on the seventh day of the week in many religions, began.

So ended the first seven days of Adam and Eve on Urantia some 40,000 years ago.

You can see some similarities between your traditional creation story and this first, most wondrous week spent in the Garden of Eden by Adam and Eve. Only mere tidbits of truth have remained, after thousands of years of retelling.

All went well for a while, as Adam and Eve did their best to settle affairs on Urantia. They had begun to develop trade relations with the world outside the Garden, slowly unfolding their plan to introduce a new, peaceful culture between all peoples.

Things looked promising at first, but establishment of law and order on a planet as far off course as Urantia would take much patience and time. Adam strongly desired to create a world government, under a representative group control, but the moment he began to implement these ideas outside the Garden, he was met with avid resistance. This resistance was in place due to the machinations of Caligastia. At the time, Caligastia had already been stripped of all power as Urantia's spiritual and cultural leader and he no longer ruled your world; however, he had not yet been removed from it. He still held deep influence over the people, though he was invisible to all but Adam and Eve.

The people clung to the lessons of "personal liberty" as taught by the leaders of the Lucifer Rebellion. It was all humanity had ever known, and all you had ever been taught—that you were separate from God, separate from each other, and to unite in any way would mean giving up your personal freedoms and liberties.

Acceptance of your inherent Oneness and global cooperation of all living things is the norm and commonly accepted way of living on other developed planets not involved in the rebellion.

It was impossible at this point for Adam and Eve to teach the people that, in fact, the opposite is true: to reunite with the Father and each other is to return to your natural state of being. In this state, your minds are at ease with the world and each other, knowing that to harm another was to harm yourself. This mindset brings inner peace and unforced goodwill towards all other human beings. To understand your Oneness is to regain all your personal power. When you rejoin your mind with your Creator and each other under One Power, you erase the idea of separation, which is what makes you feel anxious, weak, depressed and alone. It is the idea of separation that produces resistance in you towards any type of world union of all peoples and cultures.

It is because of the teachings of separateness from Caligastia that the people of Urantia are so guided by the ego today. He taught all you needed to know about conflict, revenge, hate, and selfishness.

CHAPTER 26

The Failure of Adam and Eve

BETH:

What caused the actual default of Adam and Eve from their mission here? What exactly did Caligastia do?

MARTHA:

This much about your biblical tale is true: Eve underwent a great temptation and failed. However, it was not the temptation of a "forbidden apple" that was her downfall, but rather the temptation to speed their plan for Urantia along more quickly than circumstances allowed. Though her intentions were greatly misguided, they were also very good.

I will relate this story as succinctly as possible, but know there were many moving parts involved over a lengthy timespan of some decades.

Eve began the process of integrating her violet blood with the Urantia natives far sooner than she should have. She was tempted, through insidious, undetectable means by Caligastia, to have a baby with a mortal man.

Caligastia knew the inner desire of Eve's heart; that she desired progress at a quicker pace for the people of your world. She knew you suffered and yearned to hasten the process towards the goal of world peace and illumination.

As previously stated, at that time, much of the world existed in abject spiritual darkness. The Garden was surrounded by tribes of people at war with one another, though Adam and Eve were making steady progress at establishing good relations and trade with a few of them. It was indeed a strong, albeit slow, beginning and would have succeeded if they had only had more patience.

Again, aside from teaching spiritual truth to the world, a large part of their plan had been to integrate as much of their biologically upgraded "violet blood" to the human race as possible.

Such intermixing of the genetically upgraded violet blood would give humanity immunity against nearly every conceivable disease you suffer from on your planet today. It would also have extended your natural lives by several hundred years. These and many other more subtle physical advantages would have been introduced to your people had the full mission of Adam and Eve been carried out. Yet, even though the plan failed, they were still at least partially successful, and humanity gained some of their enhancements.

Instead, their mission was compromised by the nefarious plans of Caligastia. He convinced a local leader of an influential tribe to wear down Eve's resolve to wait to intermix their genetic material with the Urantia natives. The point of waiting until there were enough members of the violet race to spread evenly throughout all tribes was to prevent an outbreak of vicious rivalry among them. If the biological upgrade was spread evenly throughout the people, no one tribe would be allowed to have a genetic advantage over another, and thus dominate them unfairly. It would prevent world war.

And so, Eve's great mistake was in the attempt to bypass this Divine Plan through coming up with her own alongside it; one she thought would simply enhance the Divine Plan already in place—although unbeknownst to her, such a plan was heavily influenced by Caligastia.

According to her plan, she would create a child with a mortal man, whose tribe would then be closely tied to the Garden people through the bond of shared kinship, thus expediting peace and unity between them.

The mortal man she chose to procreate with was named Cano, and together they created the first child of mixed blood who they named Cain. It was hoped that this child would one day become a great leader among his people, helping Adam and Eve to usher peace and civility ever more quickly into the world.

Let it be noted that there was no romantic love between Eve and Cano—this act was done out of strategy and careful planning. Many people of Urantia today may frown upon Eve for "cheating" on Adam, but the act itself was not looked upon as wrong—outside the Garden, the traditions of the local people permitted multiple children from multiple fathers. This practice was accepted as normal. Marriage, as you understand it today, did not exist. Aside from this, Adam and Eve had a relationship that transcended the physical, a bond that could not be severed by sexual contact with other beings. They were a created pair for all eternity. Nothing could ever change this status, much less creating a child with a human.

The far more serious error made by Eve was deviating from the set plan, and not having the patience or the trust in it.

As soon as conception took place, all celestial beings who were watching closely and assisting with the mission of Adam and Eve felt something go wrong. Adam felt this disturbance as well and sought out Eve to speak with her about it.

Upon meeting up with her he heard her entire story; how she had long been tempted to speed the integration of their violet blood through procreating with a human, and her transgression that had just occurred.

While they stood in the Garden beneath the Tree of Life discussing the ramifications of the situation, a voice came to them from the Tree.

The voice was not actually God Himself, but that of an archangel, the guardian of the Tree. Her name was Solonia, and whenever Adam and Eve had partaken of the Tree of Life in the past, it was her job to remind them of their noble purpose on your planet, and how important it was not to deviate from the set plans. She had often warned them that if they defaulted on their original plans, that they would lose their immortal abilities on Urantia and become as a human and thus go through the death process as a human.

Now she spoke for the last time, announcing to the pair that Eve had indeed disobeyed their covenant. She would now be stripped of her immortal status and become destined to die in a body, thus joining the ascension plan with the rest of the mortals living on Urantia.

Through Eve's transgression from the Divine Plan, Adam and Eve had failed their mission on Urantia.

Understand, Eve's was not a rash decision. Every time Adam and Eve partook of the Tree of Life, Solonia had counseled them and warned them about the serious consequences of diverging from the divine plan.

And Eve had long considered these previous warnings of Solonia and had brought these warnings up to Cano. He did not grasp the deep import of them, however, and reasoned that, since their intentions were pure, the deed would be overlooked.

He assured her that their plan was of the highest motives.

This all may be very well and true, however, even as innocently as it was executed, it still departed from the right and fair way, as was predetermined by the Divine Plan set in place.

Adam was disappointed in Eve, and thoroughly heartbroken over the failure of their mission. However, he could not bear the thought of going on alone, indefinitely in an immortal existence here on Urantia, without his beloved Eve. If she defaulted and would die a mortal death, then out of his immortal love for her so too, would he commit the very same act, and join her lot.

It was with this premeditated plan that Adam set out the very next day to find a mortal woman of high genetic bearing to impregnate with his seed. He settled on a highly intelligent woman who taught in the Garden schools.

And in the aftermath of such decisions, the most feared outcome would soon take place.

Civil war quickly broke out.

The Garden dwellers were outraged. After all the work they put into the Garden, the blind faith they put into the plan Adam and Eve laid out before them, and all the generations of dedication, these plans were ruined by an act that took but only a moment. They felt forsaken, and the blatant unfairness could not be overlooked. They were angry with the outside clans for their interference in what they were working towards, so many of them left the Garden and made war on a nearby settlement. This settlement was not the one from which Cano hailed, and many innocent people died. However, during this first conflict, Cano was among those who lost their lives, as he was still in the vicinity of the Garden when this took place.

Vengeance is blind and indiscriminate, and eventually news of this attack and the death of Cano reached his home settlement, and his people made ready to march down to the Garden with the intention of destroying it.

It was time for Adam and Eve to make a hasty evacuation of the most beautiful place on earth.

The children already produced by Adam and Eve did not go unaffected. At this time, they had been in the Garden for some one hundred and seventeen years, so they had many by then. They, too, were overcome with grief over the default of their parents.

It was at this time that Adam became so distraught he left the Garden, unannounced, without saying where he was going or when or if he would be back.

Upon the discovery of his disappearance, Eve was overcome with grief. Adam did not return for 30 days, during which time she did not know if he was alive or dead. The time of his absence was the most excruciating and sorrowful of Eve's entire existence on Urantia. Anything she experienced after this time paled in comparison to the sense of loss and pain that she suffered while Adam went missing. And her joy at his return was never eclipsed by a happier event during their time together as mortals on Urantia.

BETH:

Wait, I have a question if I may please interrupt you for a moment. How is it Eve had no idea where Adam was for 30 days? I thought they had a telepathic link. Wouldn't she always know where he was because of this connection?

MARTHA:

A very good question, indeed, my dear. Yes, they were able to communicate through telepathic means, but let me clarify for you that such communication is one-way unless both parties are in a state of mental receptivity—a state of loving peace. When either communicant becomes un-receptive to such communication, one can call and call but remain unheard by the one to whom such love is being extended. And so it was, that though Eve searched for Adam with her mind, extending her loving thoughts of communication to him, the distraught Adam was in no frame of mind to hear her.

Understand, such is it between yourself and your Creator for much of humanity's time spent on Urantia. Your Source and Center extends His unconditional love to you unceasingly, and yet few are in a state of mind to receive such loving communications. Your Father Creator never ceases to extend His love, and it is our goal to enable humanity to become aware of such calling, and so transform your minds that you are at long last able to hear and receive His tender ministrations and joy. The beloved prodigal Sons and Daughters of God will indeed one day hear their Father's call to them to come Home, returning to paradise.

CHAPTER 27

The Evacuation of the Garden

MARTHA:

Adam did not come to Urantia to make war, but to bring peace and civility. So, without delay he made preparations to evacuate the Garden and reestablish his and Eve's teaching in another location. They were to flee and not fight. Some 1200 Garden inhabitants left in a great caravan, together with the celestial couple—now made mortal—in search of a new home.

And so, contrary to your biblical records, Adam and Eve were never forcefully cast out of the Garden as punishment from God. However, choices they made of their own will triggered events that necessitated such an evacuation. Though the conditions were set by themselves, they were nonetheless undesired.

On the third day after their caravan left the Garden, they were visited by celestial hosts. These were transport angels sent to retrieve whatever children of Adam and Eve who so desired to end their physical adventure on Urantia, since the original mission had failed. Being a part of a plan that now required them to experience a substantial degree of suffering was not part of their original agreement, and therefore, they were being offered a one-time opportunity to make the choice to leave such a situation.

All children age 20 or older were offered this choice, and those who were younger were automatically taken up by the transport angels. Those children who chose to remain would become as mortals, along with their parents, since the Tree of Life was no longer available to them. Though they would live out the remainder of their years as mortals, their lives would be extended well beyond that of the average human.

About two thirds of the children opted to leave with the transport angels.

This was a sorrowful day for the couple as they tearfully bade temporary farewell to their children who were to follow a different ascension path than their own. Though they knew they would one day be united in spirit, the parting of the physical was still as difficult as any human loss. The parting was especially bittersweet for Eve in that she knew the road before them now would be long and difficult and was relieved in part that some of her children would be spared the toil and suffering that lay ahead.

And so, with heavy hearts, the caravan marched onward, after the transport seraphim departed with so many of their precious children.

However, during this celestial visitation, they were also brought some good news.

The archangel Gabriel himself came to deliver the verdict of their situation. Though they had failed in their original mission, they were not held guilty for joining the rebellion, which was still ongoing at that time. They may have been deceived in their thinking, but theirs was a mistake, not a willful action taken against God as an act of rebellion. Their hearts, though mistaken at the time of their actions, remained rooted in love and goodness. They were not being viewed as having joined Caligastia and the Lucifer Rebellion.

This was wonderful news to Adam and Eve; in that they did not know their current status as divine emissaries and what their new choice had brought them. On any other planet not involved in the Rebellion, they would have immediately been made aware of their spiritual status, but since Urantia was cut off from the universal circuits that connected beings throughout the superuniverse, they had no idea what had evolved.

As such, this was wonderful news for the downhearted couple. The only real repercussion they had generated by their actions, was the degradation to mortal bodies.

Let it be understood that their new mortal status was not punishment. It was simply the direct result of a choice made by Adam and Eve, who were now merely experiencing the consequences of that choice.

Theirs was a mistake made by many a human throughout the history of Urantia—the lesson in patience is a difficult one indeed.

In many instances, if an individual exerts enough patience, often-times what is first perceived as potential failure becomes a great success.

In light of the failure of Adam and Eve to carry out their original plans—rejoice! Many failures can be corrected, reversed or evolve into scenarios with an even greater spiritual benefit. Such has been the case with Urantia. You are now living on a planet where unique and rare opportunities for growth exist nowhere else in the entire superuniverse. Beings are literally knocking down the door for a chance to be a part of the glorious transcendent awakening about to transpire on your world. Your ascent from abject suffering and spiritual darkness is upon you now. Your world is about to undergo a transformation that has never been seen on any planet thus far. You are each a part of a process that will be told about and learned from for all eternity by an entire superuniverse!

CHAPTER 28

The Second Garden

MARTHA:

The caravan migration took almost an entire year to reach the location Adam had in mind for the second Garden. This was one of the alternate choices when the decision for the first Garden was being considered.

During this long and arduous voyage, both Eve and the woman Adam impregnated gave birth while en route. Though Eve suffered during labor, she was able to survive and successfully gave birth to her son Cain. Unfortunately, the woman who gave birth to Adam's child died during labor. She gave birth to a daughter whom the couple named Sansa. Eve took the child and raised her as her own. And so, these two half-human children, Cain and Sansa, were raised side by side.

Circumstances were harsh, food was scarce and living conditions were meager, while on this long journey.

Though your histories have been edited to exclude such information, Sansa grew up to be an outstanding individual. She contributed much to the advancement of humankind. Cain's life on the other hand, took a much sadder turn.

After reaching their destination at long last, there was much work to be done. The first Garden had been partially prepared for Adam and Eve, but this second one had to be built from scratch, though it was already inhabited by people. Thankfully, the previous inhabitants fled the region without any resistance. As soon as they saw the large caravan heading their way, they simply left and moved their village elsewhere.

People back then greatly distrusted other tribes, in that often such a march towards them meant death and war. It was much wiser to flee first and ask questions later.

Though they found the area already vacated, the current

structures and surrounding region were wholly undeveloped for their way of life. They had to build new homes and till the soil for crops. Everything had to be done from the very beginning, using sweat and backbreaking work.

Less than two years after their arrival, Adam and Eve had a son, named Abel. He was the first child born to them in the new garden and he grew up to be a herder, while Cain chose to pursue agriculture.

Due to their differences in life paths, these boys appeared to have struck up a sort of competition; both arguing many times about the merits of each choice of vocation. They had frequent heated arguments about it, because in those days, it was customary to make offerings to the priesthood and Abel insisted his animal offerings where much preferred by the priests over Cain's vegetable offerings. He mocked Cain relentlessly as both the one with superior offerings—and of superior pure blood, being the full-born offspring of Adam and Eve, which Cain was not.

Cain tried to point out that in the first Garden, the people were traditionally vegetarian; that his offerings were in keeping with the original ways taught, and thus just as worthy as Abel's meat offerings.

Abel refused to agree and continued to savagely tease and taunt his older brother.

In the first Garden, Adam had, with high priority, sought to discourage all ideas of sacrifice of any kind. It was a needless waste of food and precious resources. Such offerings appeased no one, but were simply to feed the priests themselves or to lie in rot at the altar of a God who wanted aught but loving communion between Himself and those of His creations.

However, the second Garden posed a bigger challenge. Adam was overburdened by the new responsibilities of starting the settlement over and had little time to devote to such non-essential things. Survival became the top priority. And so, he left it alone for the time being and focused on establishing basic order and living arrangements.

Without the direct leadership of Adam, the native people,

who also influenced Adam and Eve's children by sheer immersion, quickly reverted to their old ways, and re-established many of the rules held long before Adam and Eve arrived on your planet.

And so, Cain and Abel's declining relationship went largely unobserved by their parents, who were much preoccupied with their more pressing tasks. Their conflict continued to escalate without the intervention or knowledge of either Adam or Eve.

These two boys never had a peaceful relationship. Again, besides taunting Cain about the lesser quality of his offerings from the field, Abel also made sure Cain was keenly aware of his lesser bloodline, being only half of the violet race. Abel flaunted his pure blood status in front of his half-brother at every opportunity.

This fostered a deep resentment, and eventual hatred, in Cain for his younger brother, which began to fester over the years. One day Cain could take no more, and during a heated argument, out of blind rage, he killed his brother Abel in his fury; he picked up a rock, threw it at Abel striking him on the temple, causing him to fall unconscious. During this time a blood clot formed, lodged in his brain and brought about his death within an hour. He never regained consciousness.

The people of Urantia know from your own experience that much more goes into character development than mere genetics. Environment also plays a large role. Had these two boys been born under less strenuous familial conditions, theirs would have been an amicable relationship. Cain and Abel would have developed into entirely different individuals. Under ideal conditions, the best of both children would have risen to the top of their personalities, and they would have become men of great wisdom and deed.

This is just one example of the importance of the love, nurturing and attention children need in order to foster the best in them, which in time will always win out over the baser animal tendencies inherent in your physical existence.

Therefore, it must be carefully taken into account that Cain's life thus far had not been the happiest.

The first twenty years of his life were spent living as essentially the physical symbol of the default. He felt personally responsible as the reason they had to leave the Garden in the first place. Had he never been born, none of what happened would have taken place. Of course, no one outwardly blamed him for this, but he knew the history of his making, and still sensed subconscious resentment in those around him and deep shame for himself. As children often do, they blame themselves for the mistakes of their parents. In this, Cain was no different from many children today. He felt tremendous guilt for the actions of his mother, Eve, though it was no fault of his own.

After Adam and Eve discovered the death of Abel, they were reminded again of their poor decision to prematurely mix genes with the humans of Urantia. This was just one aspect of the myriad of problems they were warned would happen if the violet blood were not evenly and fairly distributed.

In light of Abel's murder, Cain had decided he should leave the second garden.

His parents supported this decision, though they did not truly want him to leave. But knowing how symbolic he was of the default, and how hard his life had been living among the original Garden dwellers thus far, they knew it was Cain's safest option.

It may seem preposterous to some of you that Cain suffered no punishment or severe retribution for his fatal act upon Abel. Here I ask you to understand that it is neither healing nor helpful to cause such a tortured mind further suffering through punishment. Rather, it was understood that Cain's act of violence was a deep cry for help and release from his long mental anguish. Adam and Eve clearly saw this though many others did not understand. The best that could be hoped for in this situation was the rehabilitation of their son through exile—a fresh start.

And so, Cain went to a land far from the second Garden, and there became a man of great leadership and courage. He did much to bring peace and trade to the savage tribes living in that region. He also later married a woman of high intelligence and beauty and named their first son Enoch, whose name is mentioned in your biblical records.

All told, Adam and Eve produced 105 children before they left your planet—53 daughters and 52 sons. Over the years, these children went out into the world to disperse as much of their pure violet blood as possible among the Urantia natives. They did this as fairly and evenly as they could, attempting to leave no people untouched.

This may sound like an astonishing number of children, but keep in mind that, though Adam and Eve had been stripped of their immortal status, they were still granted an unusually extended life due to their superior genetics—even without the aid of the special nutrients from the Tree of Life. Adam lived until he was 530 years old, eventually dying of what you might simply call "old age." His body became entirely worn out. Eve had died 19 years earlier, at the age of 511, from what you would term as heart failure, however, a more appropriate assessment would be that her heart finally broke from the burden of carrying the pain of having triggered the default of their mission.

Adam and Eve left you with as many children as they could, and as hard as it may be to imagine, you would be a lot worse off if there had been any less. Even so, you received tremendous gains from what little of the violet blood was given the world races.

What never became established during the time of Adam and Eve was the development of one world language, knowledge about the superuniverse and its inhabitants, and the true nature of God in relationship with yourselves. However, though delayed, this information and such changes are currently taking place on your planet now, approximately 40,000 years later.

As each succeeding generation passed and their blood became more admixed with the native peoples, the lifespans of the long-lived children of Adam and Eve became decreased to what you now consider normal today. Many other beneficial characteristics still linger, though are greatly reduced. At one time, people carrying one fourth or greater of the violet blood could plainly see and hear celestial beings, such as angels and other spiritual assistants in your dimension.

Think how different your world would be today had Adam and Eve been successful in their mission! In fact, they would still be living among you today, until your final destination of planetary translation into the dimension of Light and Life was complete.

Be that as it may, so ended the careers of Urantia's bestowed Material Son and Daughter, Adam and Eve.

BETH:

What a thrilling, epic tale! Is there a way we can tell if we carry any of the lingering genetic material, what you call "violet blood" from Adam and Eve?

MARTHA:

There is, and your genetic testing techniques have become sensitive enough to detect it; however, I will not reveal the means to you. It would cause a great sense of "specialness" in many of you, and thus promote the type of separation among you which we want to dispel. Suffice it to say, that there is a high probability that nearly every surviving physical body today carries at least a small amount of the genetic material from Adam and Eve.

Do not try to judge how much violet blood you carry based upon your physical attributes, such as eye color, skin tone or body type. Such physical characteristics are so diluted and intermixed now, that they are no indication of how much genetic material one carries from so long ago.

However, you will find evidence of it within you, as many of your cultural and spiritual developments reveal where much of the genetics still shine forth. The children of Adam and Eve had greatly advanced your arts, interest in science and math, as well as music and mostly, the desire to seek a spiritual connection to your Creator. Those who participate in or even merely appreciate such endeavors carry more genetic material of the violet bloodline than others.

Even so, know this: the second Garden constituted one of the greatest epochs of your human history. The Garden flourished for over 20,000 years, and sent emissaries out around the world up until as recent as 8000 to 6000 B.C. I assure you; no people and no culture have gone unaffected.

BETH:

Well, 6000 B.C. wasn't that long ago in geologic terms. Where then is this second Garden today? What's left of it?

MARTHA:

Sadly, this era ended due to territory conquests of the other surrounding tribes of peoples. Being wholly non-warlike, the residents of the second Garden were eventually simply forced to leave due to these outside pressures. These people invaded due to increasing droughts in their highland pastures; they needed new territory for their grazing animals. Being in possession of a multitude of tamed horses, they had a distinct advantage over the people of the Garden. It finally fell due to the fact that they continually sent out their best people to populate the world with their culture and superior genes, while the surrounding people continued to grow stronger.

Because of all this change, combined with war and social turmoil spanning thousands of years, there is nothing left today of the structural remains of the second Garden in Mesopotamia.

What was not sacked by raiding, the climatic changes of the planet finished off. Great floods washed across the land repeatedly for several thousand years, due to a geologic rise in the mountains around the Mediterranean area. The last trace remnants of the second Garden were completely erased by such floods, just as the remnants of the first Garden lie beneath the waters of the Mediterranean Sea, near the eastern end.

No new Garden was ever established anywhere else. The last people who remained of the original Mesopotamian culture, dwelled along the mouths of the rivers between the Tigris and Euphrates. They were called the Sumerians. But, by 6,000 B.C., their genetics and culture were already well mixed with the surrounding peoples.

Therefore, you can now no longer tell who's who as far as being a descendant from Adam and Eve is concerned. What small amount of genetic material they endowed to your races is now so diluted it is nearly untraceable. As stated above, suffice it to say that because of the spread and mixing of the races you most likely all have some traces of uplifted genetic material within you.

I would like to add a side note here regarding your upcoming open contact with races from other planets. Among the races that will be "coming out," some will appear exactly as Adam and Eve were described here: as tall blonds with stunning blue eyes and flawless beautiful features. These people are from planets that were not part of the Lucifer Rebellion and had successful Adam and Eve bestowals. Their advanced, gentle race thus bears the mark of the violet blood genetic upgrade. You will know them when you see them.

CHAPTER 29

The Era of Light and Life

BETH:

> All this about Urantia's spiritual history sounds like a fantasy story. It's almost too much to believe!

MARTHA:

> Is it any more difficult to believe than your biblical story that the world was created in seven days? Or that Adam and Eve were the first two human beings from which all others sprang? However, it must be clear to you by now how such pieces of the previous story you had, came to be. It was largely false, but still contained fragments of the greater truth. The world, creation and spiritual progress all proceed with logical pace and means in truth. What you did not expect was for God to actually make sense and for life to proceed in an orderly fashion. Strangely, this idea is the one most people will find difficult to accept.

BETH:

> I think you're right. We expect mystery, confusion and unanswerable questions. This is how we've lived in the past. But what you have laid out is an organized process for the spiritual development and evolution of humanity. I actually take comfort in knowing that someone somewhere actually knows what they're doing and we're all in good hands.

MARTHA:

> Better Hands than you could ever imagine.

BETH:

> It's disappointing to know that Adam and Eve failed to complete their mission here. I really wonder what life would have been like if they had succeeded.

MARTHA:

> Urantia would have become a dramatically different place. As previously described, when an Adam and an Eve arrive on a world,

besides spiritual enhancement, one of their main goals is racial integration—a blending of the planetary races into one, through the mixing of only the best genes from each race with the violet blood or advanced genes from Adam and Eve. Again, this process upgrades your immune system and mental capacities. You become more disease resistant, intelligent and what some would call "psychic."

This process does not begin until the progeny of Adam and Eve reach a number sufficient to spread equally among the races of the world. However, on a typical planetary visitation, Adam and Eve themselves never procreate with the natives of that world. This was a unique situation on your planet. And typically, the progeny of Adam and Eve do not go out themselves into the wide and dangerous world to spread their superior genetics, but rather, the various native tribes would send emissaries to the Garden for intermixing. Only those with the highest intelligence and most superior genetic qualities would be selected and sent forth as such. This is a voluntary effort and it is considered a great honor to be selected for procreation, a process much like the selection process for your Olympic sports.

This intermixing of the races then ends the racial wars that are typical on most planets up until this time in their spiritual history. All races unify under a new social occupation: striving to increasingly better themselves so as to qualify for admittance into the Garden. Again, the most apt comparison is to think of such a process as similar to how people on your planet train for the Olympics, excepting that efforts in intellect are also included with physical conditioning. It becomes a worldwide, ongoing effort by all people, as anyone can qualify from any social status.

Once a match is forged between one of the progeny of Adam and Eve and a native Urantian, the couple would be thoroughly educated, and then leave the Garden and return to the native's tribe. Their children would then go on to continue to intermix their genetics with the rest of the tribe.

Once this process of intermarriage begins, a new era commences on the planet: the Age of Light and Life. As a whole, the planet then begins to make a giant leap forward in social, physical, intellectual and spiritual development.

On most worlds, the Garden itself is maintained as a historical center for teaching and education, as well as a reminder of how far humanity has come, it's present state and where it is headed.

Since Adam and Eve failed to carry out their entire mission on your world, as a people you will have to arrive at such a place of peace and unity through your own means. Being without a planetary Adam and Eve, you must learn to rely solely on your own inner direction: the Voice of the Holy Spirit. However, you are not entirely without help. You still have the aid and assistance of many angelic helpers, as well as a host of extraterrestrial beings who are anxiously awaiting your readiness for their open contact so that they, too, may offer what they have learned. And there is also the promise of the return of our beloved Christ Michael to your dear forsaken planet. Therefore, you have much by way of guidance—so fear not! You will make your planetary spiritual transition with plenty of support and love surrounding you at all times.

Even so, this is obviously a much longer path than that of a normal planet, as many of you still cannot hear or refuse to believe that such guidance as the Holy Spirit exists within you and even less so the awareness of the host of unseen beings that await your acceptance of their help. However, the superuniverse is confident you will one day attain the era of Light and Life, and that all such developments as must need to, will come to pass.

The goal of every world of time and space is the attainment of the era of Light and Life. This time in a planet's future has been called the time when Heaven comes to Earth, for it is an age when time ends, and eternity begins on a world.

The entire planet is literally transformed and no longer resembles what it once was. The frequency of existence makes a dramatic upward shift.

Once attained, this era continues indefinitely on a world, truly becoming eternally "heaven-like."

The first thing that happens, once a planet enters the era

of Light and Life, is the endowment of a special temple on your physical plane of existence, to serve as your world capital. This temple is given to a world as a sign that the entire planet has completed its lessons in light and love.

This temple is not actually "brought down from Heaven" but rather, it is built out of worldly material, and brought together using supernatural otherworldly beings, and their powers to control physical matter.

BETH:

What is this temple used for?

MARTHA:

It is not used for worship as you might imagine. It is a place of communion and communication, as well as profound and sacred ceremonies of righteous spiritual passage and achievement.

It also has the purpose of a new and unique process, one that we on my own planet are about to engage in. It is the place where a physical being can translate from one reality into another. It is a place of great gathering of loved ones as they see one of their beloveds translate directly from the physical into the non-physical. It is the new means through which you will leave your bodies henceforth. Gone will be the days of mournful death, disease and slow decay of the physical form. Rather, it will be a glorious event, filled with laughter, cheers and well wishes. It is a joyful grand ceremony, indeed, as the participant receives recognition for their loving achievements and contributions to society while they walked the world in physical form.

When the body is transformed from material into the eternal realm, there is a great flash of light within the temple as the ascending mortal achieves fusion with the Divine within them. The souls that directly translate or transform from the physical into their new, "spiritual body" through this means, do not have to travel through the seven mansion worlds after physical death. Instead, they bypass all these learning stages altogether, but then later return as teachers on the very mansion worlds they bypassed. Therefore, they continue on their inward journey towards Paradise right alongside the rest.

By the time the age of Light and Life has come, a planet has long since adopted one world language, one religious belief system and one race of people.

Though this may all sound quite fantastical and farfetched, understand that such developments are the normal progression of most planets who have not fallen under difficulties such as your own. And yet, I tell you, this future still awaits Urantia and it will be all the sweeter because of what you have endured and overcome.

The attainment of the age of Light and Life is the pinnacle of achievement for all worlds existing in the material reality. This reality contains no poverty, crime, insanity or diseases. Art, science and culture reach unprecedented, unimaginable heights. Society shines with the beauty of its grandest achievements on all levels of experience.

Gone are all forms of war, and there is no need for any type of police force as all people have become self-controlled and self-governed through listening only to their own peaceful Inner Guide. Life for everyone becomes simple and uncomplicated. Technology and spirituality are equal on the highest level possible on a material world, and everyone enjoys a life filled with joy and deep satisfaction.

Until you translate into the realm of eternity, you will remain mortal on such a world. You will continue to breathe, eat, sleep, and drink, as this stage of living is not yet quite Heaven, but it is a level of reality most closely related to Heaven, while still in the physical.

However, besides better immunity and near nonexistent disease, advanced races of light and life also enjoy better vision and hearing, as well as an extended lifespan.

By this time, the population has also become stationary society has taken it upon itself to regulate its numbers so as not to overpopulate their planet. My own people have been doing this for some time now.

What you will enjoy most however, is your new ability to clearly communicate with your inner guides, such as the Voice of the Holy Spirit and angelic helpers. This will greatly enhance their ability to be more effective guides to you.

All this and more awaits humanity's future, as you slowly progress on your path together.

CHAPTER 30

Making Sense of Life

BETH:

I'm having trouble making sense of all this and keeping it in perspective. I feel as though my whole belief system and what I understood about God, life and the afterlife have been completely disassembled and reassembled into something new I need time to figure out and accept.

MARTHA:

I will try to help you tie all this together, to simplify the information so that you can more easily assimilate all that you have learned.

You have a famous saying on your planet by the man William Shakespeare: "All the world's a stage, and all the men and women merely players." This is a fairly accurate analogy, in that while here in this reality you do not know who you really are; not as God created you to be, but rather as you imagine yourselves to be. You are each playing a pretend role. However, this is where the analogy ends. This is because, contrary to what is true in a play, life here in this seventh outer ring of existence in time and physicality is not a set role with pre-determined lines. In a play, you must stick to the words of the script and use only those props which are in alignment with the story. No allowance is made for individual creativity, change in character or spontaneity. Only the growth and changes written into the storyline are allowed. The actor would be kicked offstage by the director if he or she suddenly took personal liberties with their own character.

Instead, a much better analogy would be to compare your current existence with children playing make-believe in a sandbox. Children playing as such imagine new roles for themselves at every turn. Their world can shift and change as they decide, and anything is possible. One day they can build themselves an intricate sandcastle, while the next they can form a pile of rubble and be just as pleased. They can shift from villain to hero in a heartbeat, being equally satisfied by the experience of both roles. They have full control and total personal freedom to choose who and what they want to be in relationship to one another while playing in the sandbox.

Such is your experience now. You are in a world where anything is possible—including your full release from it. Your present character is merely one you made up, and you can change it or accept your real identity at any time. The only thing that must be done to escape the sandbox entirely is to wake up from the idea that the sandbox is all there is. Currently you believe it is your home, rather than a temporary place where you can act out whatever your mind imagines.

You would tell a child they were foolish indeed if they refused to leave a sandbox at the end of the day, insisting it was where he or she now lived and also refused to give up the imaginary identity they gave themselves.

Yet this is the situation you find yourselves in now. You find it difficult to give up this imaginary world at the end of each lifetime, returning here again and again, trying to establish it as real and insisting that your happiness can be found in what is not eternal. Eternal happiness can only be found in the eternal realities. This is what you each must ultimately come to choose.

In light of your situation, let us clarify all that has been shared here in this work in a unique and special way; let us concisely summarize your existence in the physical from start to finish. This will deepen your overall understanding.

And so, my dear friend Beth, living on the world of Urantia at this time, in its "sandbox stage" of spiritual development, I ask you to present the information you have been divinely given in the form of a play. This is to marry together both analogies—that of being actors in a play, but not on a stage; you are all truly merely playing make-believe together in one big sandbox.

CHAPTER 31

The Sandbox

Cast of Characters:
THE HOLY TRINITY
GOD: Father Creator
CHILD: Son (All of humanity)
NARRATOR: Holy Spirit

NARRATOR:

In the beginning there was God. And God created a Child to share in Union with Him so that He could experience relationship with Himself as His Own Love. One day, this creation of God, His Only Child, had an insane idea. She wanted to know what life would be like if she were the maker of her own world, separate and apart from God. And God, being a good Father and the giver of unconditional love and free will, conceded to this wish, though God warned the child that she would suffer from this choice. However, nothing could teach the child this, for suffering cannot be taught to one who knows not what it is and has never experienced it. And so, in ignorance and foolish desire, the child proceeded to make a world unlike Heaven...

CHILD:

Father, I would like to make a new home and would like to live there instead of Heaven. I make this choice only because I would like to try to make something on my own, using only my will, not in Union with Your Will. I would like to try being my own creator.

GOD:

My dear child, if you do this, you will have to forget Me. For you cannot have both worlds, you cannot live in two places at once and have awareness of both. You make a grave error in doing this; you are choosing to separate from Me, and this choice will cause you unwanted suffering. However, I know you will not understand this unless you experience it for yourself. And so, you may use Our Great Power to make that which I am not. You may separate from your Union with Me in order to know what it is to be what We are not. Know this though; you cannot truly separate from Me, for it is impossible. I am That Which gives you Life and without Me you would cease to exist. Therefore, this will merely be an imagined separation and you may return to Me at any time of your own choosing. No real harm can or will be done by your choice to separate—there has and only ever will be one choice: Union with Me, God your Father in Spirit, Giver of your Life and True Identity.

NARRATOR:

And because she was just a child, she was given a sandbox to play in and all she could build was an impermanent sandcastle. A simple plaything that would never last for all eternity; but she cared not about this, for her memory, understanding and experience of eternity had been blotted from her mind, in order that she be able to make the sandcastle to begin with; for as God had said, she could not have both worlds. Such is the sacrifice for choosing to experience separation from God—the only alternate experience to Union in Him.

CHILD:

Wonderful! I have made a sandcastle. This is my new home and I willingly choose to forget all that I Am and where my true Home in Heaven so that I can have this experience here. I know I must do this in order for my experience here in the sandbox to be real enough to be believed. For if I do not believe in what I have made, then I have made nothing.

NARRATOR:

What the child did not understand was that she had, indeed, made a world of nothing. It would not last, because it was not eternal. This was the best she could do on her own, for when one tries to make a world opposite to what God Wills, one cannot make anything eternal; for God only Wills what is eternal. On her own, she could only make that which would one-day end in time, for God is timeless, and God can create only what is not bound by time. And so, in this moment, time came into existence as the alternate experience to God's timeless eternity.

CHILD:

And now I would like to live here in my sandcastle. I cannot do this from a state of Union with God, and so I must separate my Identity into parts. I will divide my Oneself into bodies that appear separate from each other in order to live in this world of separation. Otherwise, I will not believe in my own self-made world. I must not have any memory whatsoever of my Union with God lest I give up my own endeavors here and return Home. I am determined to do this by myself.

NARRATOR:

And so was born the idea of the ego and separate bodies in which it could live. But upon doing this, the child soon became beset by a great many problems. This is because she made a choice in opposition to what was the truth. The truth is, God is One in peace, and she had no other choice but to choose the opposite of God's peace, which is separation in conflict. And thus, a world of conflict arose as the only possible alternative.

CHILD:

Father, I have a problem!

GOD:

Yes, my dear child, I hear your prayer. What is it you need help with?

CHILD:

So many things threaten to wipe away my home. Will You please do something to stop such disasters? Everything here is unsafe and unstable in the sandbox. I feel fear at every turn. Nothing in this sandbox seems to last.

GOD:

My dear child, this is the nature of the world you made, and you chose this conflict as the world in opposition to My peace. Therefore, there is only one solution to your conflict: return to My peace. In order to have My peace you must give up your beliefs in your false reality and return your belief to Me. I am your Creator; you did not create yourself and cannot create anything real without Me. Come Home, dear child, and forget this foolish place, this sandbox. I Call you from within to remember Me.

CHILD:

> I cannot hear You, Father. Nor do I remember You or what Heaven is like and therefore cannot believe in any of it wholeheartedly. There is nothing here to compare with You or Heaven, and so I doubt that any of it even exists. My attention will remain here on this world of conflict, as a distraction from my remembering You, lest all that I have worked so hard for be taken away. I do not want to give up any of it. I am determined to find joy here in this sandbox, no matter what the cost. I will sacrifice nothing I have made.

GOD:

> The price you are paying is steep, dear child. The sandbox is costing you your peace and happiness. In keeping it, you sacrifice everything. But nevertheless, I will continue to unceasingly Call to you until you are satisfied this world cannot bring you any measure of true satisfaction and you turn, at last, within to hear My Voice and remember Me.

NARRATOR:

> And so the child carried on with her life, and as each problem seemed to be solved or faded away, another always arose to take its place; just as sand unceasingly moves, changes and blows in the wind, she experienced a relentless parade of difficulties that made little or no sense to her. Because of this, at times she even felt punished by God, Who of course loved her unconditionally and understood her self-inflicted predicament and would never do such an unthinkable thing to His child for simply making a mistake. Yet neither would God take away what she had made, for God respected His child's wish to keep the sandbox.

CHILD:

> Father, though You seem to not hear my prayers, I have another problem. I would like certain people to love me in certain ways. I want a partner and children and good parents. I want everyone to love me in the manner of my choosing. Yet no one ever seems to do what I want. They hurt me at every turn and cause me endless suffering. I seek love but cannot find it. Please help me find love; but I want love in the manner of my choosing.

GOD:

> My dear child, you have chosen to forget that love makes no special arrangements. Love IS. True Love is uncompromisingly equal in Its giving. You cannot demand that it do only your bidding because it is equally given to all. You will forever be disappointed by such special relationships, as your heart breaks each time your demands of others are not met. For each of you want conflicting things. In order to have peace in your relationships, you must give up your false beliefs in what these relationships must be and return your belief to My One Love that unites you all. You are still My One Child, though you see yourself as separated. All such needy, fear-based, ego-love relationships simply reflect your lack of Love for your Oneself. Love makes no demands. You see all others as separate from you and refuse to acknowledge My Love that unifies you together. And so, you suffer from the sight of such separation. While you ask for such special relationships to be real, you ask for suffering, and though it breaks My heart, you will receive what you have asked for. Such is the law of giving and receiving—the law of Love.

NARRATOR:

> And the child did not hear or understand such a response and so she carried on with all her messy relationships, trying to piece them together and make them fit an ego-ideal that would never work because God's Love does not give special favor. Special relationships will always bring pain, but if given to God to be made whole, they flourish under His peace, acceptance and mercy. For the ego, it is impossible to love as God Loves, but if one learns to give such relationships to God to Love through them, they will be transformed. To receive love, it cannot be chased, for this means you see it as something outside yourself to be sought after; and you will always chase it away. Love must be welcomed from within with peace and not taken by a sword, for Love makes no demands. It is already part of your Oneself. And so, when you truly give love, you will truly receive it, for such is God's Law of giving and receiving.

CHILD:

> Father, You still seem to not be listening to me, but I want another thing. I would like a nice home and a good income to live a comfortable life. I do not want to live in poverty or have to go without those things I think I need in order to be happy in this world. I pray to You to give them to me. If You loved me, you would answer these prayers.

GOD:

> My dear child, there is nothing in your sandbox world worthy of Who You Are. Giving such things is to give you nothing; for it is a make-believe world you invented to maintain your separation from Me. You ask Me to give you nothing, and though it breaks My heart, it shall be yours. However, understand that you will not be satisfied with any of it. Having or not having nothing, is still nothing.

NARRATOR:

> The child had yet to understand that a world built upon sand will not last, and though you can heap more sand upon sand, it is still but sand. Having more of it may satisfy for a short while, but it will still wash away.

CHILD:

> Father, I pray to you for yet another thing, though I cannot see or feel You anywhere. I want to be well liked and highly respected. I want a place of power in this world. I want to be the best and have the most. I want awards, recognition and status. Let me be the victor of all I choose to attempt and accomplish in this world. Let me fail at nothing here. I want to be the greatest among people. If You loved me, You would answer this prayer.

GOD:

> My dear child; you have built a kingdom out of sand. It is foolish to come to such a place and believe it is real. Would you truly want to be crowned king of the fools? I tell you this: In a world of fools, it is best to be the least. Therefore, seek instead to be the least in the world of fools and you will be counted amongst the greatest in Heaven. Seek My Kingdom instead and you will find the majestic grandeur that you so desire and know to be your

true world, your True Inheritance. Only My Kingdom is worthy of My One Holy Child. Do not seek to be king of the fools, lest you achieve it.

NARRATOR:

Power, fame and glory are the temptation of the ages, and few escape its delicious pull into darkness. To see others succeed while one feels like a failure in comparison is the comparison of the ego to other egos. In God's Kingdom there is no comparison, for Love is equally given to all. No one is less and no one is greater than another. And so, All is given to All and All are satisfied in this state of joy and gratitude. To desire to be "more" is merely to find less, for you will align with the mindset of the ego's idea of separation and not know your true glory and power in Union with All. Therefore, do not seek to become king of the fools, but rather, celebrate those times you are the least fool among fools—in fact your apparent "failures" are often your greatest successes. Those who seek to be least in this world will find themselves first in Spirit, when they align themselves with God's Will, Who Is First Cause. In Him, there is no order but One, and all are First within Him.

CHILD:

Father, nothing seems to ever go right, and if it does, it does not last for long. And now my body ages and fails me, as well as those I love. I want our bodies to last, even though I know the body is just like everything else here in my sandbox world. I know it will one day fail each of us entirely and die, and even though I understand this, I still pray to You until the end, that it lives on. Please answer this one last request! Do not let death or sickness come! The pain of the loss of the body is just too great to bear!

GOD:

My beloved child, I would not have you suffer so. This is not My Will for you. I created you as eternal and you cannot truly die. All suffering is but at your own hand, only because you have chosen your own will and your own way alone. You have chosen to believe you are this body. Come, take My Hand and I will lead your mind away from this darkness and back into My Kingdom where all the Heavenly Hosts will rejoice at your glad return. Nothing has happened to your place here with Me. I have kept your True Self safe and whole and resting in My Peace this entire time. You have only imagined that you left Me. Be healed of all guilt and fear over having gone so far away. You have made a journey without distance, for you cannot truly leave Me and My Love or you would cease to be. I am That Which Sustains you for all eternity; and so, all was forgiven even before you made the choice to forget My Love. Awaken, dear child, and hear My Call. Come Home. You are not a frail, weak body. You are Love's Grand, Eternal Creation. This is the truth for each and every one of you. No one has been forsaken, left behind or is ever truly gone. All are united with All for all eternity. Be at peace and know this to be true, despite what happens to your bodies.

NARRATOR:

And at last something within the child began to stir; an echo of a Voice she recognized was dimly heard. She had tried, lifetime after lifetime, to find happiness in an endless variety of ways and found no lasting joy. Yet she could faintly remember a Joy that surpassed all others. This is what she so desperately sought. All have been Called by Something deep inside that whispers of a Promise made by God that they would one day return to Him, united once again. This whisper took hold within her and she began to turn more and more to listening to this Voice within, instead of seeking outside herself for peace; for life in the sandbox was indeed the opposite of peace. And in order to complete her transition from life in the sandbox back into the Light of God's Love, she must next learn how to let go of everything the sandbox means to her. For many, this transition is a painful process that appears to be filled with sacrifice and loss; but this need not be if the process is properly understood from the outset. In fact, it is undertaken with great joy by the heart that is prepared to let the world go. Know that all trials are but lessons one has failed in the past, presented once again so that a better choice can be made to escape all pain forever by forgiving the world they made.

CHILD:

I have tried everything, Father, and though I crave Your peace and Love, I search and do not find it. What am I doing wrong? Where is Your peace? I am tired of this sandbox. I am unhappy and at the bottom of the lowest of all places in my heart. What must I do? What do You want from me that I may be happy? I am willing to listen now and do exactly as You ask.

GOD:

Up until now you have played a child's game in a false world. Then when this world did not work out the way you had planned, you asked Me to intervene and move the false reality around to suit your liking. You have asked Me to "fix" your world but have repeatedly rejected My Answer. This is because My Answer has not been one to your ego's liking. My Answer is thus: it is time now to set aside such childish games and grow into adulthood. I ask only one thing: That you forget this place, this sandbox; forget your identity in it and the identities of everyone there with you. Forget what you think the purpose of anything is, for you do not know; you have forgotten Me and believed in the sandbox instead. Forget the sandbox world now and remember Me. Forget all you ever thought you knew about the world around you and let My Voice write the truth upon this clean altar in your heart. For then you will have at last made room for your forgotten memories of Me, and you will also remember your true Home in Heaven. Simply remember you know nothing as it exists in truth and the truth will be revealed to you.

CHILD:

I am ready to do as You ask Father, but I know not how to do this. Such terrible thoughts about the world clutter my mind at all times and it seems impossible to be rid of them. This sandbox and all its problems seem to command my attention and drag me down. This place seems so real! Please tell me how to clean my inner altar of all this darkness! I no longer want any of it! Father, I am so desperate, I'm willing to try something new. I ask that only Your Will be done and not my own. What is Your Will, Father? I would do it now, for I am lying in a heap of my own misery and troubles and know not what else to do. And so, I would reach out to you, offering You my service, instead of asking You to serve me. In the past, I have only asked for Your help, in the form of my prayers. Now I am truly willing to try something different. I would like to give instead of take—now I want to help You. I want to give something to You, instead of asking something from You. I would learn that to give is to receive and so I give to the highest Source: God Himself. So, I say again, let Your Will be done and not my own, and let me serve You in what You Will. What is Your Will, Father?

NARRATOR:

At last, with this plea, the child had finally prayed a real prayer. One that God could truly answer. She had stopped telling God what to do. Instead, she was ready to let go of all she ever knew about everything she had ever known, and desired that it be replaced with God's Will. All prayers before this had simply been her ego's way of "nicely" telling God what to do; mere petitions asking for particular outcomes to a myriad of problems, needs and wants. When one prays in such a way, one is choosing to lead instead of follow. Such prayers are always answered but the recipient will feel unheard and abandoned because they chose to continue on alone, under the guise of prayer, ever asking God to do as they command. The only way to be released from this cycle of desperate needs and wants is to give over all needs and wants to God, by ceasing to tell Him what to do and how to do it.

The prayer that triumphs over all needs and wants is this:

Father, let your Will be done and not my own, for I do not know who I am, what I should be doing or what the world is in truth.

Because You know the truth of all things, I ask that You teach me Your Will and how to love my brethren even as You love them.

I am not here to ask and to take; I am here only to give and serve You Who sent me and to be truly helpful to You in what You Will.

Amen

And with these words, one will effectively resign as one's own leader and step back and let God lead the way.

CHILD:

> Father, I feel an inner shift! You have lifted my burden of solving all my problems on my own and You have solved them all for me by making them obsolete. They do not exist! This world is not real, and I now know it in my waking mind, and a mind awake knows of its truth in Your Unity and with All Creation. I am awakened to my Oneself, United with my Creator and at One with every aspect of Your Creation! I will cease to try to harm others with my thoughts, words and actions, because I now fully understand they are a part of Me. And neither will I fear them, for again, You are within them and we are One. Together, We are limitless in Our power and Our peace. And with these realizations, I carry Your peace into the world with me as a beacon of strength and light, healing all those you send me, healing the world. I am at peace as I rest in Your deep, abiding Peace. My heart is still in the Grandeur of Your eternal, joyful Love. There is now nothing in this sandbox that can cause me fear, suffering or pain. My joy is as absolute, unchanging and unshakable as Yours, for I now share your Vision of Light.

GOD:

> And now, dear child, with your relinquishment of your own will and joining with My Will for your peace, the conflicts of the sandbox world will fall away from your life and be replaced with My Peace. And so, this is the beginning of your experience of My Heaven on Earth as you continue to live an extraordinary life, extending My Grace, Love and Peace to the world and all you encounter on your journey. The obstacles to your peace have been lifted, and if you seem to falter on your way, as you finish your time in this world, those problems too, will be lifted the instant you remember to call upon My Peace. Be blessed and made whole as you continue living your joyful life through My Peace, and abiding joy will be your only experience. And when the time comes for you to truly leave your sandbox experience behind you forever, you will leave your body by your own choice; not by waiting for your body to die, but rather by gently setting it aside because its usefulness is done. Yes, child, you will transcend even death and resurrect to new life, even as Christ once demonstrated how to transcend

from your sandbox world.

NARRATOR:

And from that day forth, the child never feared the sandbox world again, for she knew the truth of its existence—or lack thereof. It was not her true home, nor anyone else's. If anyone decided to "throw sand" and cause misery and conflict, she knew she had but two choices: she could either "throw sand" back and cause further misery for herself and others or decide to leave the sandbox altogether. She chose to leave. She left the sandbox by withdrawing her belief in it. Each time it tried to draw her back with its "realness" she simply reminded herself it was only a child's game and sometimes children throw sand at one another in order to get what they want. Nothing could truly harm her Divinity in God the Father. She fully understood there was no such thing as "good" or "bad" people in the sandbox—only those who were aware of their Unity in God's Love and those who were not. Knowing this truth, the child rested in the peace of extending only God's Love to the world. Soon, all trials fell away; her life yielding to only what was peaceful and good, for all error in thinking will always yield to love if it is brought to love and not willingly hidden from it. Only the good, the beautiful and true will come into the life of one who heals everything by extending God's Love and Light to All That Is. Such is the law of giving and receiving: to have, one must give all Love to All, and nothing but love and happiness will be returned.

And so, God's Will was done on earth. Forgiveness of the original error of separation was made complete. Peace and unity were restored to all minds joined in knowing they were One Mind, One Voice, and One Name Created together by One Love.

And the vision of the sandbox world was gently and peacefully washed away from the mind of the child and replaced with the real world of Heaven.

Again, this miracle can truly be achieved by simply never forgetting how to reignite the truth in your mind through words such as these:

Father, let Your Will be done and not my own.
For I do not know who I am or who or what anything

in this world truly is.
Therefore, I cannot judge it.
Let me know Your Will instead, that I may carry it out
with You, the One Who Knows the truth of All Things.
I am here only to be truly helpful to You Who sent me.
Let me learn to give and to bless, knowing that
what I give I shall also receive.
Therefore, let me join Your Will in loving my
brethren even as You do; as part of my Oneself.
Then shall the world be forgiven, and all will be healed.
Amen

Thus, the Child learned to follow instead of lead and truly demonstrated the power of the law of love: that giving and receiving are One in truth. You will receive as you have given, and so choose to give maximally: give all your love to God and all those He sends to you—your beloved brethren One with you in Him. In doing this, you are serving God through fulfilling His Will for you to serve and love everyone, even as He does.

Nothing real can be threatened.
Nothing unreal exists.
Herein lies the peace of God."
A Course in Miracles Text.Introduction.2:2

Therefore, do not fear the sandbox—nothing in it is real!

This story is my own and ours together. I lovingly walk the remainder of this journey with you beside me as all of humanity awakens, for I cannot go alone; we are One Love. Now we go together, you and I; we willingly leave the sandbox behind us forever. Soon we will know only the joy of God's Love for all eternity, as He Wills.

I love you unconditionally.
—Beth Geer

AFTERWORD

My E.T. Close Encounters
of the
First and Third Kind

What I am about to share are two recent encounters I had with extraterrestrials of the first and third kind since the completion of this book. The first encounter was of the first kind: a UFO sighting over my home. The second encounter was of the third kind: an extraterrestrial visit in my bedroom about a month later.

I am sharing these events simply because I am deeply compelled to. It is my strong feeling that it's time to prepare humanity further mentally for open contact with beings not from earth, in the very near future. These two peaceful encounters will hopefully help ease some of the trepidant feelings many people may still have towards first-hand contact with extraterrestrials. And as events unfold in the future, I will continue to share all my experiences publicly. It is time we fully accept their very real presence and open our minds to the grandeur that lies just outside of what we think is reality.

Close Encounters of the First Kind:
A UFO Sighting

On Wednesday, November 17th, 2021, I arrived home from work at 6:00pm. Upon entering the front door, I asked my husband if the dog needed to go out for a bathroom break. I figured that since I was already dressed for the cold it would be convenient for me to take her.

We live out in the country on a 40-acre hobby farm, with a wide view of the sky. As Freya and I headed down our quarter mile driveway, I looked up at the large, bright moon which would be full in two more days.

I was struck by something odd about it. The sky was dotted with large clouds, and the moonlight shone through them, which was not unusual at all. However, what got my attention was that I saw what appeared to be three moons in the formation of a large triangle.

I marveled at this as I walked the dog down our long driveway, not feeling any fear at all, but rather, trying to figure out how the moonlight was reflecting behind the clouds in such a way so as to appear to be three equally bright lights.

My dog and I returned to the house at 6:15pm, just 15 minutes later. I had kept my eyes on the lights the entire time, and they had moved only slightly, tilting a bit, which caused them to appear to be slowly moving away. I still believed the phenomena I was seeing was an optical illusion caused by the moonlight behind the clouds. I was so nonchalant that I didn't even bother to take a picture with my phone. I'll never again make that mistake.

However, it did occur to me that these 3 lights reminded me of a large spacecraft. So, as sort of a humorous gesture purely for my own amusement, I mentally sent a message to any extraterrestrials on board the "spacecraft" that I meant them no harm. I also told them that I would do my best to not be afraid of them, should they ever come down to meet me in person. Then, in what seemed to be my own imagination, I received a mental response back from them, that they would do their best not to frighten me or be afraid of me either. I felt a loving sense of peace from this "imagined" exchange but thought nothing of it. I went on with my night, not even bothering to mention any of this to my family.

I truly didn't believe I saw a spacecraft hovering over my house!

Later that night, at about 8:00pm I was rinsing the dinner dishes in the sink and looked out the kitchen window. There, just coming up over the trees, was the real moon. This shocked me to my core because that meant it wasn't even visible in the sky two hours prior when I was out with the dog. What were the 3 lights I had seen earlier then? I ran outside to check if the lights were still there, and of course they were gone. I also noted that the moon was not yet even close to where I had seen the lights. I realized what I'd seen had to be some sort of craft flying in the sky. Some people have suggested it might have been a military drone or plane, but I don't think so.

First, it made no sound. Second, the span between the three lights was immense. If an average airplane is about 50 meters long, then this craft had to have been at least a mile or two across. It was absolutely gigantic. This was the main reason I believed it was moonlight reflecting off the clouds in the first place; I couldn't believe anything else in the sky could be that big. Perhaps the government is manufacturing aircraft this size in secret, but I personally feel this was something not made by humans.

Close Encounters of the Third Kind:
An Extraterrestrial Visit

About a month later, on Tuesday, December 28th, 2021, I went to bed like any other night. I had no idea that I was about to have an encounter with beings from another dimension right there in my bedroom.

I "dreamt" I woke and looked at my clock, which read 3:30am. I say "dreamt" because what follows, felt like a real experience in our "normal" reality, but through the lens of a dream-like mental state.

I looked over at the wall adjacent to my side of the bed. It seemed to shimmer in a way that made me think it had become transparent; like a hologram you could walk through, but still looking exactly like a solid log wall. (We live in a log home). The holographic opening appeared to be about the size of an average human.

Next, six extraterrestrial beings walked single file through this "portal" in my bedroom wall and surrounded my bed. They had large dark eyes, no hair and wore no clothing. Their bodies were about the size of an average human, and their skin color was a mix of greyish-bluish-green. Physically, they appeared genderless and identical, but I could sense individual personalities among them and that some were male, and others female.

My husband was still sleeping soundly in the bed beside me, while I was on my back, half propped up on my pillows watching the strange procession. As this event took place, I felt no fear. I don't think I had time to, for these beings got right to work, sending me some form of "energetic healing" that caused me to move into a state of blissful loving, peace and gratitude. In fact, I felt sublimely euphoric throughout the whole encounter.

Two extraterrestrials stood at the foot of my bed, standing like statues, and could feel them sending me loving energy directly from their minds. There were two more stationed directedly next to me on my side of the bed, and two others on my husband's side, for a total of six. The ones standing on the sides appeared to be facilitating the energy flow with intricate hand motions over our bodies. I felt grateful for this energy for I could feel it was healing something in my energetic field. I knew they were helping us in some manner.

This went on for some time, and once complete I made a mental exclamation that I couldn't believe I wasn't afraid of them. I felt just the opposite in fact; I wanted them to stay. They felt like loving family to me. I could feel their love not only for me as an individual, but for the whole of humanity. They joined me in this thought, equally amazed and happy I was not afraid of them. They then said, "Yes. We allowed you to witness this process for a reason. You passed the test. We are very pleased you do not fear us."

They then filed out of my bedroom, back through the portal in my wall just as they had arrived.

The next thing I knew, I was "aware" of a spaceship directly over our house. I couldn't see it, but I knew it was there. I was then "told" telepathically that evil aliens had placed a bubble of harmful gas around our house, and that this gas was going to interact with the carbon dioxide from our breath and our fireplace, causing an explosion that would annihilate my home and family.

Alarmed, I mentally cried out for help, wondering what to do, or how to escape. In response to these thoughts, I "heard" the "good" aliens in my mind, instructing me to open all the windows in the house, to let in fresh air which would foil the plans of the evil aliens.

I hesitated at first, because it was currently the dead of winter and extremely cold outside. But I decided to trust the message I'd received and went around my home, opening all the windows.

Immediately upon completion of following this instruction, the evil aliens revealed that they were in fact not evil at all, but rather, the good aliens in disguise, testing me. This time, they were testing to see if I would trust them enough to follow their instructions, even if such instructions ran contrary to the logic of the world–such as opening all the windows of my home during an extremely cold winter night.

They next informed me that I had passed both tests: the test of fear and the test of trust. I did not fear their bodily forms, and I trusted that they were there only to help me and would not lead me to harm.

They then told me that those who did not fear and who trusted would make the transition easily. Others who did not, would not make the transition at all, or would have a more difficult time with it.

I asked them what "transition" they were talking about, to which they answered, "The interdimensional shift of your race and planet to a higher vibrational existence."

I then "woke" my husband within this dream-like experience and told him all that had just happened. His response was to go check the portal in the wall, to see if it was still there. So, we got out of bed to do this, agreeing that it was unsafe to have a holographic opening in our wall someone could fall out of. Our bedroom was on the second story, so a fall could be fatal.

My husband ran his hand over the portal opening and it passed right through–it was still there. I then called our two teenage children to our room to explain what had happened and warned them to be careful of the opening in the wall. It looked solid, but they could easily fall right out.

At this point, I wondered what exactly was on the other side of the wall? I decided to take a chance and poked my entire head through, expecting to see nothing more than the cold winter night and our backyard.

That was not what I found.

Once I put my head through, instead of a cold shock of winter night air as I expected, my face was met by warmth, and a panoramic view of vast deep space, filled with stars. My heart instantly filled with joy and excitement. I pulled back out and told my husband and kids that they absolutely had to put their heads through and look at what I saw. It was simply amazing!

So, my husband decided to check it out first, to make sure it was safe for the kids to look and cautiously ran his hand over the log wall before putting his head through. It was solid once again. The portal had closed.

I decided to go look out our bedroom window, to see if I could catch a glimpse of their spaceship or anything else. The extraterrestrials then informed me telepathically that I would not be able to see their spacecraft, as it had never entered our reality.

But they did leave something behind for me to see.

As I gazed out into our backyard, I could see hundreds of small crop circles dotting the landscape, each about the size of a circle you could make with your arms. And as I looked closer at them in the moonlight, I noticed each circle was vaguely heart shaped, filled with a multitude of spiral patterns inside. These impressions were in the inch or so of snow we had recently received in "real life." In fact, everything in this dream-like experience was true to life. There were no distortions or irregularities that normally occur during "regular" dreams, and everything progressed in a clear, logical order. In all honesty, this dream-like reality and my "normal" waking reality were nearly impossible to tell apart.

As I gazed out at the heart shaped crop circles, I understood they were a symbol of love and trust from the extraterrestrials. A parting gift, expressing their good intensions and desire to assist me and the rest of humanity through our upcoming transition into a new reality.

I then reentered our current physical reality—the one I was used to and called "normal." The clock read 5:00am and that was the end of my experience. The only phenomena I was left with, was that I could feel (and still can!) a degree of the loving euphoria I experienced during the extraterrestrial's visit simply by recalling any part of the dream-like experience.

Later that morning, I checked our backyard for the crop circles, but found none. And when I asked my family if they remembered anything unusual from the night before, none of them recalled anything out of the ordinary about their night's sleep.

In conclusion, I feel this was not the first time these visitors have come to my room in the night, and I believe they have been visiting many of us for a long time.

I also feel this experience is only the beginning and has been given to me to share with others to help them prepare for what's to come. May the world be ready for the upcoming spiritual transition or "interdimensional shift" to a new reality, or what some call the 5th dimension. May all of humanity be fearless and trusting of those who are here from other worlds to lovingly help us move into the New Earth, a reality where we will all coexist side-by-side in a happy, peaceful, lovingly amazing world.

> "Beyond this world there is a world I want. I choose to see that world instead of this, for here is nothing that I really want." —A Course in Miracles Workbook 129.7:3-4

> "It is impossible to see two worlds which have no overlap of any kind. Seek for the one; the other disappears. But one remains. They are the range of choice beyond which your decision cannot go. The real and the unreal are all there are to choose between, and nothing more than these." —A Course in Miracles Workbook 130.5:1-5

"BONUS MATERIAL"

My Visit to Planet Neba

As I type these words, this book is now only about a week away from the printers and I'm rushing to include this one last "Martha adventure." I feel this event is just too interesting and wonderful not to share. I struggled with where and how to include it, when Martha came to the rescue. She said, "Put it at the very end as a succulent piece of bonus material for the reader to enjoy. Our parting love gift to each one who took the time to read our story cover to cover."

And so here it is dear reader. Enjoy and thank you!

Sometime mid-June of 2022, I had yet another of my vivid, out-of-body, lucid or "waking" dreams. This one took place on planet Neba, the home world of my interdimensional companion and dear friend, Martha. And as Martha has previously stated, this is a place not physically reachable from our dimension of time and space. We are simply not in the right density required to even be able to physically see her people, much less physically travel to their planet.

According to Martha, we humans are currently of the 3rd density, though rapidly moving through the 4th level now, and we will quickly go on to settle for a while in the 5th density. This is all part of our awakening process. Martha and the people on her planet exist in the 9th through 12th density. They are in the last stages of transcendence. Each density has its own corresponding reality and as we move upward, we are able to see and interact with greater types of beings.

However, despite all this, apparently higher densities can indeed be reached when one is not in their physical body at all. And so, unbeknownst to my waking, physical earthly mind, my higher mind decided one night, to try and visit Martha where she lived. Here is what I experienced:

I found myself in the middle of an ocean; not drowning or swimming, but rather, being carried along, cradled in the arms of a "squid-man"—one of Martha's people. He swam at an amazing speed, almost unbelievable, with his upper torso completely out of the water, while his legs pumped below. He seemed to swim like this effortlessly, even when I was being carried in his arms like a child. Only my lower back and bottom just skimmed the surface of the ocean waters, occasionally splashing me a bit. The water was warm and relatively calm, with only a few gentle waves.

His features were much like Martha's, and, just like Martha, I found him extremely beautiful. In fact, I felt deep love for this being, and could feel that love being returned to me by him. It was a shockingly powerful love. And for a moment, his love felt directed specially towards me alone. I wondered, "Who is this man and is he in love with me?"

Then as I had this thought, my understanding broadened—facilitated by the squid-man himself, as he explained to me telepathically that he loved all living things in this intense way. That such love radiated from him naturally and is felt by all who enter into his presence. In fact, he explained, all his people the Nebans love this way, openly extending the all-inclusive love of Creator to all. To a human, this is remarkable because we cannot feel such love in the presence of one another as do they.

I thought that was wonderful and felt no less special. In fact, I felt gratitude that I was included in his love of all.

I then asked him why he was carrying me through the water.

He replied again telepathically, "Because you traveled here astrally and landed in the middle of our ocean, about ten earth miles from the nearest shore. You had to be rescued. You do not have the strength to swim this far alone. And even if you could, there are many things that would eat you."

This comment was a surprise. I had no idea why I was there in the first place, how I had arrived, or where I was swimming to. I had no memory of travel or my decision to come to Neba astrally.

I observed my rescuer as we swam on, smoothly, never losing momentum. I could not put my inside left arm around his shoulders or neck to hold on. His dorsal fin was fully extended from his spine to the top of his head, as he swam with his full strength. This fin stuck out about six inches along his back and between his shoulder blades, then tapered to just a few inches high as it reached the top of his head.

Since I could not put my arm around his neck, I settled for just hooking my hand around the top of his shoulder from behind to help him carry my weight. His build was slender, but he seemed extremely strong. His long thin, webbed fingers gripped me securely, but gently.

I asked him how he was able to swim with only his legs, while carrying me and keeping his torso halfway above the water.

He replied, "Do not forget that Martha told you our seas are a third more salty than your home world. This increase in salinity adds buoyancy. We are not as heavy in the water as you think."

Even so, I wondered how he could swim so smoothly with such power and speed. There was no sense of him pumping his legs in a flutter pattern or any other type of undulating "fish-like" movement.

He "heard" my thoughts and replied, "I am actually running underwater."

"What!?" I thought back. "How is that possible?"

"Is this not how your ducks swim smoothly across the surface of the water on your planet? I am taking great strides with broad feet underneath the water. This causes us to glide seamlessly, like a duck gliding across the water. There is no break in momentum when swimming in this way."

Oh! I thought. That made total sense. It would have never occurred to me that a humanoid would swim in this fashion.

I then looked out towards the horizon and saw only endless sea, but soon a long straight landmass came into view. As we approached, I could make out thick vegetation and a white sandy beach as far as the eye could see in either direction. There were no discernible buildings or signs of inhabitation. Everything appeared perfectly natural and serene.

Then as we came closer, I could make out forms on the beach. About twenty or so squid-people were standing along the shore, watching our approach. They were a mix of adults and children. The adults ranged in height from about six to eight feet, and the children were all about four feet tall. I remembered Martha telling me that the children were born in "batches" on the same day and therefore would be close to each other in size.

Then the water gradually became shallower and my rescuer was now swimming much slower, and would soon be touching bottom. Another squid-man walked out to meet us. He was a full foot taller than my rescuer, broader and much older though he seemed to be robust and strong. I felt he was a leader.

He took me from the arms of my rescuer and began to carry me, walking through the water.

I asked him, "Why don't you just put me down?"

Again, all communication continued to be entirely telepathic.

He replied, "Because the water here is still too deep for you. It will come up to your neck and shoulders."

"But I can swim very well. I trained to be a lifeguard on my world," I told him.

And he said, "It is rude and uncustomary to make a landfaring guest swim for their travel, unless it's for pleasure. It is our responsibility to make sure you reach land safely and comfortably. Not to mention something could still eat you at this point, though we keep these shallow waters as safe as possible for our young."

He finally put me down and the water came up to only just below my knees.

That was when I looked down at my feet to see if I was wearing shoes, wondering whether they were going to get wet.

To my delight, I was barefoot.

Then immediately to my fright, I noticed that my entire body was bare. I was totally naked! Where were my clothes!?

I stopped dead in my tracks for a moment to process my embarrassment. And instantly the whole tribe along the shore assured me telepathically that my natural, uncovered bodily state was perfectly fine with them. They understood my concern. They pointed out to me that they too wore no clothing, though they did not have the exposed sexual parts that we humans have. None of this mattered to them, and they made this very clear to me. With these reassuring thoughts and an overload of love flooding my mind from them, my embarrassment vanished, and I forgot all about my nudity.

In fact, the next sensation had my full attention: I felt the sand beneath my feet.

It was exquisite! It was the finest, softest, whitest sand I'd ever seen. I can only describe it as feeling like I was walking on powdered sugar, except it was not sticky. In fact, it seemed to prefer to cling to itself, rather than my skin. It was like walking on air.

I asked what type of material it was made out of.

A tribe member replied, "It is a mineral not found on your planet, eaten by many sea creatures, who then expel it in this refined state after consumption."

So, I was walking on purified fish pooey?

The tribe found my realization amusing, but also reminded me that much of my home world beach sands were made through a similar process.

I then asked the names of my rescuer and the tribal leader. All I received was a melodic vibration I could not put a human name to, though I tried. They explained that their names were a vibration that would not translate directly into a human word. But, since they knew that we humans do assign numbers to our alphabet through the use of numerology, and that such numbers carry vibrations and are assigned particular qualities, each squid-gentleman chose a letter from our English human alphabet that was a close vibrational match to the essence of who they each were. Roughly speaking, my rescuer said I could call him "D" and the leader could be called "H."

(I later found that the letter "D" in numerology is assigned the number "4" which stands for a stable, determined, dependable person. And the letter "H" is assigned the number "8" stands for authority, inner wisdom, social status, and confidence.)

I stood there on the beach looking at the circle of beautiful squid-people gathered around me, each emanating that same deep, all-inclusive love as did my rescuer "D."

I carefully scanned over them, looking for Martha.

"Where is Martha?" I asked.

"She is not here," H replied. "She is over 2,000 of your earth miles away, deep inland."

"Can you bring her here?" I asked. "Or can I get to her quickly?"

"No," he replied. "Martha will not come, and we will not bring you to her. This is only because you are not supposed to be here at all. She will not encourage such visits before you're ready. That is why you landed out in our open ocean and not directly in her presence. You do not yet understand how to astral travel on your own or how to control it. My child, though your visit is received with love and excitement, we need to send you back. I'm sorry."

I then felt supreme embarrassment over my unintentional transgression. I wasn't supposed to be there at all! I instantly knew my higher mind deeply wanted to meet Martha in person and had decided to try to find her through my bodiless dream-state. Apparently, I had decided to attempt to find her without knowing anything about astral traveling by myself. I felt like a child caught doing something only adults should do and failed. Like taking out your dad's car for a drive before you had a driver's license and only a vague know-how of how to operate a vehicle—and then having to be rescued.

Knowing these thoughts, again the good Nebans sent me loving, reassuring telepathic messages that no harm had occurred. It was simply a matter of me waiting for the appropriate time to visit them. All was well. I could be sent back without any issues. There was no wrongdoing and no punishment. In fact, they would never punish anyone for anything.

And so, I agreed to allow them to send me back into my earthly body, which was just fine because I had no idea how I'd gotten there to begin with, much less how to return.

They joined hands in a circle around me, and began to each hum their own single note, creating a beautiful harmony, unlike anything I'd ever heard. It made my heart swell with love for them.

I stood there in the center and closed my eyes, absorbing this lovely sound with my whole being.

The next thing I knew, I woke in my bed, with little to no recollection of this entire experience. I remembered only a beautiful, intense dream about being in the ocean, carried at high speed in the arms of a handsome squid-man from Martha's plane. I could intensely recall the love he exuded, but not any of the other details.

This snippet of a dream nagged at my mind, popping in and out over the next couple of weeks. The intensity of it would not diminish as so many dreams do over time.

Finally, on July 7th, 2022, I casually asked Martha outright about it. Was this a dream or did I really have this experience?

Her reply was startling.

"Yes, not only the small part you remember now, but much more." And with that, she began to reveal the whole adventure a piece at a time over the next few days, as well as answering my questions about it.

After "downloading" the entire story, my first question was, "Martha, why didn't you come to me when I visited?"

She replied, "Because it was not yet time for us to meet and it was the only way I could gently discourage future such visits from you. Should you continue to visit astrally, you would eventually decide to stay permanently, and while this would be allowed—we are each free beings—you would have then caused your earthly body to perish. With your life-energy transferred to our dimension full-time, you would have nothing left to live in your earth-body. It would appear to simply die of natural causes. To your family, it would appear as though you died in your sleep. Furthermore, you would then break all your current earth-life soul agreements and promises to yourself and others. The tasks you came to earth to complete in this life would go undone and such things cannot be avoided, but only delayed. This would then mean an undue long delay in your ascension plan. And this I know you would not want."

I processed and accepted this information then asked, "So what would have happened if I hadn't been rescued by D in the ocean? What if I'd drowned or been eaten by a sea creature?"

"You would have woken with a jolt from what would have appeared to have been a horrific nightmare about drowning in the ocean or being eaten by a sea creature. This trauma was something you didn't need and was completely preventable. So as soon as I became aware of your astral entrance into my dimension, I sent the Neban nearest you in the ocean to your rescue and notified the nearest tribe on the beach of your imminent arrival, and that they should send you back," Martha replied.

"Okay, that makes sense. But why did I land in the ocean? Couldn't my astral body just float to the ground right next to you?" I wondered.

Martha explained, "Usually an astral traveler is either with a guide or knows where they want to land, and lands there. You however, left without a guide and had no idea what you were doing and landed at random, ending up in the sea. And though you are a strong swimmer, you are not strong enough to swim ten miles. You only bring with you the skills you're able to extend from your current inhabited body. You're still "you" as you are experiencing your identity now, but just in a different density."

"Can I ask why I was naked? Did I forget to project clothes onto myself?"

Martha replied, "In a sense, yes. You were naked because you went to bed naked, and your mind simply projected yourself as you were. If you'd gone to bed wearing pajamas, you would have been wearing them in my dimension also."

"Good to know," I thought. "Another question. What were you doing over 2,000 miles inland? After seeing how amazing your people can swim, I can't imagine any of you ever wanting to be far from the sea. And just how big are the landmasses on your planet anyway?"

Martha explained, "I was resting at my home. Which incidentally is not far from water. None of our inland homes are far from water. We have terraformed our landmasses to be riddled with waterways and lakes of all shapes and sizes as a means to travel quickly from place to place on our planet. These waterways, rivers and lakes are not unlike your system of roads. As for the size of our landmasses, we have but one. It was once a vaguely "heart shaped" mass, but a fissure developed ages ago that split the bottom three fourths open like a clam shell, nearly cleaving it in two. It is still attached at the top by a moderate land bridge about 200 miles wide. Overall, the left side is approximately 1,000 miles by 1,500 miles and the right side is much larger, being about 6,000 miles by 3,000 miles." (To put it in perspective, Africa is roughly 5,000 miles by 4,600 miles).

"That doesn't sound like a lot of land compared to earth," I observed. "I thought your planet had about a fifty-fifty land-to-water ratio?"

"We do—our planet is much smaller than earth," replied Martha.

"That's interesting to learn. What part of the landmass was I brought to?" I wondered.

"You were brought to the long straight section of the inner right side, about mid-way," Martha replied. "The right side was nearly a clean break from its counterpart."

I had one last pressing question, "Martha, why couldn't I remember my astral adventure in total upon waking? Why did it take a couple of weeks for you to tell me the whole story?"

To which she replied, "Because it was all your mind could integrate from your adventure at the time. The experience was simply too much for your human personality to integrate consciously all at once. The experience was too foreign—you have never done such a thing before. And as you thought about the one thing you could remember about it; you became more and more open to what else there might be to the story. Then, when you were finally ready for the whole memory, you naturally thought to ask me about it. This was my indication you were ready to have all the details revealed to you."

"Oh," I replied. "This kind of reminds me of how long it takes us to remember things that happened to us in the past. Sometimes we have to gradually accept pieces of memories before we're ready for the whole truth. Except it's usually something more traumatic."

Those were all the questions I had for the time being, but I did have an observation confirmed by Martha.

I thought about how strange it was that I found the squid-people with their fish-like faces so utterly beautiful. Then I also thought of the powerful love they radiated while I was in their presence. I realized then that it probably didn't matter what they looked like, because the love one felt in their presence overrode any physical appearance they might have. They could look like piles of stacked mud and be equally as radiant.

Love truly sees beyond the physical. We are not our bodies. We are the love within ourselves. This is what we are here on earth to learn to see above all else. And once learned, we take a great leap forward in our ascension plan.

And that's the whole point of everything, I think. To learn to love beyond all appearances and feel instead the Unity we share with All Creation. I hope we can live on earth like they do on Neba someday. Heaven on earth. Martha's right. I can't go back there until I'm done here, or I wouldn't return to earth.

ACKNOWLEDGMENTS

First, I would like to thank the Holy Spirit for facilitating all communication between Martha and me, and all people and beings, seen and unseen, who helped bring these words so lovingly onto the page. I could never have done this alone.

Of course, I also thank you dear Martha, from the bottom of my heart, for your patience and teaching, your love and light. And mostly Martha, I thank you for your friendship.

I also thank my husband Paul for his support and love; for believing in everything I do and for fully supporting each step I take. You have denied me nothing and given me everything. I love you.

I also want to extend my heartfelt gratitude to my dear publishers, the beautiful team of Ronnie and Ivor Whitson and Cogent Publishing. I am truly blessed by your wisdom and guidance, grace and hard work in helping me bring these words into the world. None of this would have happened without you.

My deepest thanks to author Jon Mundy for the excellent, love-filled, and insightful foreword for this book. I am truly honored to call you friend. Your support is deeply appreciated!

And I warmly thank my dear friend Glenn Hovemann, who among many other things, is a publisher of Miracles Magazine, for featuring excerpts from my book and other writings in your magazine. Also, thank you for your enthusiastic support as I took my first tentative steps with the material of this book, unsure whether or not sharing such information with the world would ruin my life. To my extreme joy, so far readers have been kind and receptive! I also have to thank you Glenn for introducing me to author Brian Longhurst and his wife Theresa.

Which leads me to thank my beloved editors Brian and Theresa. Your expert eyes caught every detail missed and I can't thank you enough for your service. Our meeting was no coincidence. You were meant to do this work, for me and for all who need to read it.

Speaking of which, I want to thank you dear reader. Without

you my Oneself is not complete and I thank you for your Presence and your Light. You are an essential part of all creation. Thank you for being you, and for your support in rediscovering Who We Are through reading books such as this. I love you with unconditional Love.

AUTHOR BIOGRAPHY

Beth Geer's spiritual background is rich and diverse. She has had a multitude of psychic, paranormal, and deeply profound spiritual experiences—including extraterrestrial contact—throughout her life. She comes from a strong, traditional Catholic upbringing, although she no longer attends or identifies with any religious group. If asked what religion she belongs to she simply states that she is "self-taught," meaning that she prefers to seek guidance from her own Inner Teacher or higher Self, rather than follow any organized religious institution.

Beth has been a student of *A Course in Miracles* since 2004 and now actively teaches its principles to others through her online writings and books. She has also practiced tarot reading since 1993, is a Reiki Master and has enthusiastically studied astrology, numerology, and many other psychic, paranormal and spiritual arenas. Though her religious and spiritual background may appear to be contradictory, it is this very contrast that has given her an open-mindedness towards God and life.

Beth is the author of "*Awakening To One Love*: Uncover the inner peace and joy hidden within you," and is currently working on her third book: "*The Light Has Come!* Decoding the mysteries of *A Course in Miracles*," which, together with Holy Spirit as her constant Guide, she carefully and concisely explains the deep meaning of each chapter of the ACIM Text book. As a preview of the book she has converted this material into YouTube videos which visitors can view at no cost on her YouTube Channel Beth Geer.

She regularly posts her current miraculous experiences, deep insights, and latest adventures with other beings from the unseen realms— nature spirits, fairies, and sasquatch, among others—on her blog, YouTube channel, and newsletter. She frequently is a contributor to "Miracles Magazine," "The Embrace online magazine," and "The Miracle Worker Magazine;" and has been a keynote, guest speaker on the Miracle Network and its Miracle Café. In 2019 Beth was a speaker at the "Miracles in the Mountains" weekend conference in Boone, SC. She has enjoyed interviews on various podcasts, including "Sunday with Mundy," hosted by author Jon Mundy, as well as being a repeat guest speaker at the Lake Harriet Spiritual Community Church in Minneapolis, MN.

Beth lives in a log home on a 40-acre hobby farm in rural Minnesota, with her husband Paul, their two children, Miranda and Samuel, along with three beautiful horses and a varying number of outdoor cats. She is a pharmacist by day, and in her free time—when not tending to family, animals, or plants—she works on extending a message of healing and love to the world through many avenues, including her monthly newsletter "Miracle Minded Messages," which she turns into YouTube videos. In these videos, rather than sitting in front of the camera herself, she often uses footage from the beautiful countryside landscape surrounding her farm, which she feels is far more interesting to watch than her "talking head." In addition she thoroughly enjoys nature photography and videography—yet another "side hobby."

You can read more from Beth on her website: www.bethgeer.com, and her YouTube Channel Beth Geer.

Printed in Great Britain
by Amazon

85669359R00124